Romeo and Juliet

by William Shakespeare

Jane Sheldon

Series Editors:
Sue Bennett and Dave Stockwin

HODDER
EDUCATION

AN HACHETTE UK COMPANY

The publisher would like to thank the following for permission to reproduce copyright material:

Photo credits:

p. 9 Ian Dagnall/Alamy; **p. 11** Vladimir Mucibabic/Fotolia; **p. 14** david hughes/Fotolia; **p. 19** Igor Normann/Fotolia; **p. 26** AF archive/Alamy; **pp. 32, 35** Pictorial Press Ltd/Alamy; **p. 37** AF archive/Alamy; **p. 58** Photos 12/Alamy; **p. 80** Georgios Kollidas/Fotolia

Although every effort has been made to ensure that website addresses are correct at time of going to press, Hodder Education cannot be held responsible for the content of any website mentioned. It is sometimes possible to find a relocated web page by typing in the address of the home page for a website in the URL window of your browser.

Orders: please contact Bookpoint Ltd, 130 Park Drive, Milton Park, Abingdon, Oxon OX14 4SE. Telephone: (44) 01235 827720. Fax: (44) 01235 400454. Lines are open 9.00–17.00, Monday to Saturday, with a 24-hour message answering service. Visit our website at www.hoddereducation.co.uk

© Jane Sheldon 2016

First published in 2016 by

Hodder Education

An Hachette UK Company,

Carmelite House, 50 Victoria Embankment

London EC4Y 0LS

Impression number	5	4	3	2	1
Year	2020	2019	2018	2017	2016

Cover photo: © magnez2/istockphoto.com

Typeset in 11/13pt Bliss Light by Integra Software Services Pvt. Ltd., Pondicherry, India

Printed in Italy

A catalogue record for this title is available from the British Library

ISBN 9781471853661

Contents

This guide is designed to help you to raise your achievement in your examination response to *Romeo and Juliet*. It is intended for you to use throughout your GCSE English Literature course. It will help you when you are studying the play for the first time and also during your revision.

The following features have been used throughout this guide to help you focus your understanding of the play:

Target your thinking

A list of **introductory questions** labelled by Assessment Objective is provided at the beginning of each chapter to give you a breakdown of the material covered. They target your thinking in order to help you work more efficiently by focusing on the key messages.

Build critical skills

These boxes offer an opportunity to consider some **more challenging questions**. They are designed to encourage deeper thinking, analysis and exploratory thought. Building and practising critical skills in this way will give you a real advantage in the examination.

GRADE *FOCUS*

It is possible to know a play well and yet still underachieve in the examination if you are unsure of what the examiners are looking for. The **GRADE FOCUS** boxes give a clear explanation of how you may be assessed, with an emphasis on the criteria for gaining a grade 5 and a grade 8.

REVIEW YOUR LEARNING

At the end of each chapter you will find the Review your learning section to **test your knowledge**: a series of short specific questions to ensure that you have understood and absorbed the key messages of the chapter. Answers to the Review your learning questions are provided in the final section of the guide.

GRADE *BOOSTER*

Read and remember this helpful grade-boosting advice: top tips from experienced teachers and examiners who can advise you on what to do, as well as what not to do, to maximise your chances of success in the examination.

Key quotation

Key quotations are highlighted for you, so that if you wish you may use them as **supporting evidence** in your examination answers. Further quotations grouped by characterisation, theme and key moments can be found in the Top ten section towards the end of the guide. Line references are given for the Cambridge School Shakespeare edition (ISBN 978-0-521-61870-0). '1.5 137–138' means 'Act 1 scene 5 lines 137–138'.

O, I am fortune's fool.
(3.1 127)

Introduction

Studying the text

You may find it useful to read sections of this guide when you need them, rather than reading it from start to finish. For example, the section on *Context* can be read before you read the play itself, since it offers an explanation of relevant historical, cultural and literary background to the text. Here you will find information about aspects of Shakespeare's life and times which influenced his writing, the particular issues with which Shakespeare was concerned and where the play stands in terms of the literary tradition to which it belongs.

As you work through the play, you may find it helpful to read the *Plot and structure* section before or after reading a particular act or scene. As well as a summary of events there is also commentary, so that you are aware of both key events and features in each of the acts and scenes. The sections on *Characterisation*, *Themes* and *Language, style and analysis* will help to develop your thinking further, in preparation for written responses on particular aspects of the text.

Many students enjoy the experience of being able to bring something extra to their classroom lessons in order to be 'a step ahead of the game'. Alternatively, you may have missed a classroom session or feel that you need a clearer explanation and the guide can help you with this too.

An initial reading of the section on *Assessment Objectives and skills* will enable you to make really effective notes in preparation for assessments. The Assessment Objectives are what examination boards base their mark schemes on. In this section they are broken down and clearly explained.

Revising the text

Whether you study the play in a block of time close to the exam or much earlier in your GCSE English Literature course, you will need to revise thoroughly if you are to achieve the very best grade that you can.

You should first remind yourself of what happens in the play and so the section on *Plot and structure* might be the best starting point for revision. You might then look at the *Assessment Objectives and skills* section to ensure that you understand what the examiners are looking for in general, and then look carefully at *Tackling the exams*.

This section gives you useful information on question format, depending on which examination board specification you are following, as well as advice on the examination format and other practical considerations, such as the time available for the question and the Assessment Objectives which apply to it. Advice is also supplied on how to approach the question, write a quick plan, and work with the text, since all of the examination boards offer an extract-based question for *Romeo and Juliet*.

Focused advice on how you might improve your grade follows, and you need to read this section carefully.

You will also find examples of exam-style responses in the *Sample essays* section, with examiner's comments in the margins, so that you can see clearly how to move towards a grade 5 and then how to move from grade 5 to grade 8.

Now that all GCSE English Literature examinations are 'closed book', the *Top ten* section will be an invaluable aid, in that it offers you the opportunity to learn short quotations to support points about character and themes. It is also a revision aid which identifies the top ten key moments in the play.

When writing about the play, use this guide as a springboard to develop your own ideas. Remember that the examiners are not looking for set responses so never try to memorise chunks of this guide to regurgitate in the exam. Identical answers are dull. The examiners hope to reward you for perceptive thought, individual appreciation and varying interpretations. They want to sense that you have engaged with the themes and ideas in the play, explored Shakespeare's methods with an awareness of the context in which he wrote and enjoyed this part of your literature course.

The best way to enjoy Shakespeare is to see the play performed live in the theatre. However, if that is not possible, there are many film versions of *Romeo and Juliet*, ranging from the classic 1968 film directed by Franco Zeffirelli to Baz Luhrmann's modern adaptation starring Leonardo DiCaprio. You will find interesting differences from the text in every film. For example, in the Baz Luhrmann version, modern pop culture is used as a backdrop to the text and there are some variations in the verse itself. These are enjoyable versions of the tale which convey the essential message of the play but should never be seen as a substitute for the text itself. An experienced examiner is very quick to spot if a candidate has relied on a film version of the text for their revision. You need to read and know Shakespeare's original text.

Enjoy referring to the guide as you study the text, and good luck in your exam.

Context

Target your thinking

- What is meant by 'context'? (**AO3**)
- What was the source of *Romeo and Juliet*? (**AO3**)
- Why did Shakespeare choose Verona as the setting for his play? (**AO2** and **AO3**)
- What beliefs were held in Elizabethan England? (**AO3**)

What is context?

Knowledge of context will help you to understand and appreciate your reading of *Romeo and Juliet*, but what exactly is it?

Context is a wide-ranging term. It refers to the historical, socio-economic and political circumstances of the time, as well as the playwright's beliefs about those circumstances. It also refers to the way that more personal events in the playwright's own life may have influenced his thinking and writing. Finally, it may refer to developments in the play as a form which may have influenced the way it was written.

William Shakespeare

William Shakespeare was baptised on 16 April 1564 in Stratford-upon-Avon, the third of eight children. Shakespeare's actual date of birth is not known because births were not formally registered at this time in England, although baptisms were.

Shakespeare was educated at the local grammar school. He married Anne Hathaway when he was 18. They had three children: Susanna, born in 1583 just six months after her parents' marriage, and twins, Hamnet and Judith, born in 1585. Hamnet died in 1596 at the age of eleven.

Shakespeare moved to London around 1590 and was, by this time, a playwright and actor. He lived mainly in London for about 20 years, writing most of his 37 plays there. Several of his plays may have been co-written with other playwrights and some were revised by other writers.

Shakespeare died at the age of 52 on 23 April 1616. He was buried in Holy Trinity Church, Stratford-upon-Avon.

▲ Shakespeare's gravestone bears an epitaph which he supposedly wrote.

Elizabethan England and Verona

The setting

There is little mention of Verona's customs or of the qualities of Verona itself beyond the generalised description of 'fair Verona' in the Prologue to the play. In fact, the social, moral and philosophical values presented in the attitudes of the characters in the play all mirror the attitudes of Elizabethan England. By setting the play in Verona, Shakespeare achieved two things. First, he widened the appeal of the play, increasing the numbers in his audiences. Second, he deflected any accusations of being critical of the society whose rules were set down by his principal patron, Queen Elizabeth I.

The support of the monarch was crucial to the survival of the theatre at the time because, in spite of its huge popularity, there was also much opposition to it. Many Puritans (members of a strict religious movement) believed it to be sinful. Furthermore, large audiences brought the risk of spreading the bubonic plague and theatres closed for lengthy periods of time during outbreaks of the disease in the late 1500s. They closed indefinitely in 1642 but would have been shut down sooner without the backing of the monarch.

Power

Patriarchal Verona reflects perfectly the degree to which men also held power in England, even though this was a society that was ruled by a queen. *Romeo and Juliet* is set in fourteenth century Italy, which was ruled by local lords, such as Prince Escalus. In the play, the Prince holds ultimate power in Verona and is the voice of law. His name means 'scales' – a common symbol of justice – and his pronouncements are definite, representing the unquestionable power held by an Elizabethan leader, despite the play being set in another country and century.

The Prince's presence is felt throughout the play, due to his threat that death will be exacted upon anyone who breaks his rules of peace by continuing the feud. In England, Queen Elizabeth had the power to send her subjects to prison or order executions, so Prince Escalus' level of power would not be unfamiliar to an Elizabethan audience.

Prince Escalus shows leniency later in the play and banishes Romeo rather than executing him. This seems to suggest that he is an inconsistent leader, particularly as he admits that he has based his decision on the fact that Mercutio was a relative, admitting 'I have an interest in your hearts' proceeding'. This is a biased decision but, again, we must understand that Queen Elizabeth would have been able to make similar decisions about her subjects. She had to obey the laws but, as no law could be passed without her consent, was able to make the kind of decisions that Prince Escalus makes in *Romeo and Juliet*.

Feuding

In the world of the play, it is the male heads of two wealthy families of similarly high social standing ('both alike in dignity') who are involved in a feud (a long-standing quarrel, usually based on a point of honour) that seems to have arisen out of nothing more than an 'airy word'. (In other words, out of nothing much at all.) This is not incidental. Shakespeare's point in not even stating the cause of the feud reflects the degree to which male pride and a sense of honour was exaggerated at this time, leading to all sorts of unnecessary violence and agitation.

Shakespeare himself would have been familiar with challenges to his honour, after a contemporary called him an 'upstart crow' for being an actor who also wrote plays. In 1598, the playwright Ben Jonson, a friend of Shakespeare's, actually killed a fellow actor in a duel. Such quarrels to defend honour were not uncommon, although the feud between the Capulets and Montagues is particularly long lasting and far reaching, having gone on for years as an 'ancient grudge' and involving even the servants of both families.

▲ 'In fair Verona, where we lay our scene...' (Prologue 2)

Men and women

The women we see in the play are of a lower status than the men. Lady
Capulet and Lady Montague try to stop their husbands from fighting in
Act 1 scene 1, but are ineffectual. At this time, to be manly was not to put
up with any form of insult, no matter how trivial. We see instances of this
throughout the play and this is explored further in the *Characterisation*
and *Themes* sections of this guide. What is important for us to understand
at this stage is that, for Shakespeare's sixteenth-century audience, the
behaviour of old Montague and Capulet and of the young, passionate and
impetuous youths in the play would have been regarded as normal.

Build critical skills

Juliet makes a promise to marry Paris that she has no intention of fulfilling. What do you think Shakespeare might be suggesting about the male dominance common in his society and how it affects women's choices?

Shakespeare also uses *Romeo and Juliet* to explore the position of women. Juliet is strong-willed for a female of her time and much of her dialogue with the other characters shows this. At times she adopts a subservient role when forced to do so by her father, but she does defy him nevertheless. For example, in Act 4 scene 2, she tells her father that she has 'learnt ... to repent the sin/Of disobedient opposition' and will from that time forward be 'ever ruled by [him]', yet she has already made her plans to do exactly the opposite.

From a production point of view, another factor to be aware of is that, in line with the narrow choices available to women at the time, females were not allowed to perform on stage, so all the female roles were played by young boys whose voices had not yet broken. Current productions are, for this reason, often more explicit in the depiction of the love scenes in the play than the original performances would have been.

Destiny

Another important belief that is widely reflected and questioned in the play is the force of destiny. England at this time was a primarily Christian (Protestant) society and the Elizabethans held a strong belief that what happened to you was dictated by external forces that were stronger than the individual person. The vast majority of people believed not just in God but also in fate, destiny, fortune (luck) or the stars (astrology). Although most people believed in the existence of God, debates took place at the highest levels of the Church about the extent to which individuals had free will. These debates played an important role in the European Renaissance movement in the fifteenth century.

Such a common belief provided a convenient way for people to relieve themselves of responsibility for their own actions, as it was commonly believed that your fate had already been decided by a higher power. Shakespeare and other playwrights of his time who questioned the degree to which we might be able to command our own lives were unusual, and it is because questions like this are timeless that these plays are still enjoyed today. Without this contextual knowledge, we lose much of what the play is about. The Prologue immediately introduces the idea of destiny, calling the lovers 'star-crossed' and telling the audience what will happen. This suggests that their fate is already sealed and the audience just has to watch it play out. Romeo also holds this belief and has misgivings before going to the ball, sensing that his attendance will lead to a terrible end.

Key quotation

Some consequence yet hanging in the stars Shall bitterly begin his fearful date With this night's revels...
(1.4 107–109)

He is attributing the responsibility for what will happen to him to a force beyond himself and goes on to accept this entirely when he states, 'But he that hath the steerage of my course/Direct my sail!' Shakespeare is making it clear that Romeo believes the stars and some divine pilot are in charge of what will happen to him, rather than himself. In illustrating this to the audience, Shakespeare is reflecting what most of them would have believed themselves. Religious and superstitious beliefs often merged for the Elizabethans and this is frequently reflected in the actions and words of other characters as well as Romeo, throughout the play.

In Act 3 scene 5, the morning after Romeo and Juliet's wedding, Juliet questions, 'O think'st thou we shall ever meet again?' but believes that any future meetings are at the mercy of fate. Shakespeare even personifies Fortune in this scene, capitalising it and having Juliet speak directly to it, requesting that it return Romeo soon.

Her appeal seemingly goes unheard. The lovers never see each other alive again.

Source material

It is thought that *Romeo and Juliet* is based on Arthur Brooke's narrative poem 'The Tragicall History of Romeus and Juliet', but there is an Italian version of the story actually set in Verona that bears some similarity to Shakespeare's version. In the poem, Juliet is 16 rather than 13 and many of the characters in Shakespeare's play, in particular Mercutio, are entirely new creations.

It is important to realise that, although Shakespeare took the seed of an idea from another source, in *Romeo and Juliet* he moves far beyond this source in creating complex characters with human (and timeless) motivations and weaves them all together into a tale that resonates even in the different society we live in today.

Elizabethan theatre

The theatre was a popular place in the 1590s, attracting huge audiences of up to 3,000 people at a time. Attending the theatre was unlike it is today. It was a rowdy occasion, with the crowds often responding verbally to events portrayed on stage. This would have made it necessary for Shakespeare to convey his themes over and over again, through as wide a range of means as possible, including characters, events, language, symbolism and the structure of the play itself.

Beginning the play with a Chorus speaking a Prologue served as a way to get the noisy crowd's attention ready for the play. The Chorus also summarise events later in the play, in case a chatting audience had missed anything.

The Globe Theatre

Most of Shakespeare's plays were performed at the Globe Theatre in London. The audience either stood in front of the stage (these people

---

Key quotation

O Fortune, Fortune, all men call thee fickle;
If thou art fickle, what thou dost with him
That is renowned for faith? Be fickle, Fortune:
For then I hope thou wilt not keep him long,
But send him back.
(1.5 60–64)

Build critical skills

A modern audience is more likely to believe that the characters' actions lead to consequent events rather than consider that events were controlled by destiny and could never be changed.

Which characters' actions do you think lead to the final events? How might the characters' belief in destiny prevent them from making better decisions?

Key quotation

...if you with patient ears attend,
What here shall miss, our toil shall strive to mend.
(Prologue 13–14)

---

were called Groundlings and did not have to pay much to attend a play) or sat on hard wooden benches (these were wealthier people who would have to pay more to be seated).

In 1997 a reconstruction of the theatre was built on the South Bank of the River Thames between Waterloo and London Bridge railway stations, close to the site of the original building.

▲ The Globe Theatre

Literary context

Shakespeare was working in the theatre and writing plays during the Renaissance movement, which was a time of great social and cultural change in Europe. The Renaissance spanned from the fourteenth to the sixteenth century and represented a rebirth in art, science, music and literature. New work and ideas were put forward at this time and there was a great enthusiasm for fresh writing. Artists and writers became more inquisitive about the world around them and often produced work that questioned traditional beliefs, as Shakespeare did in *Romeo and Juliet* when he set established ideas of destiny against new views about free will. In this way, Shakespeare was forward thinking but he also embraced established ideas, drawing, for example, on traditional ideas of courtly love and chivalry in the play. Courtly love was a traditional medieval expression of affection, where knights courted unattainable women and pined for their love, as is shown in Romeo's affection for Rosaline.

Notably, Romeo moves on from this unproductive relationship to find true love with Juliet. Shakespeare seems to be rejecting the falsity of courtly love and presents instead a more convincing, passionate relationship for his audience.

Key quotation

She is too fair, too wise, wisely too fair, To merit bliss by making me despair. (1.1 212–213)

GRADE *FOCUS*

Grade 5
Students will be able to show a clear understanding of the context in which the play was written.

Grade 8
Students will be able to make perceptive, critical comments about the ways that contextual factors affect the choices that the writer makes.

(Note: Eduqas exam board does *not* assess AO3 – the relationship between text and context – in the Shakespeare part of the exam.)

REVIEW YOUR LEARNING

1 What is meant by the context of a play?
2 What use does Shakespeare make of the Prologue?
3 What similarities can be drawn between Queen Elizabeth and Prince Escalus as leaders?
4 In what way was Shakespeare himself familiar with challenges to honour?
5 What does the term 'patriarchal society' mean?
6 Why was Shakespeare unusual in creating some characters that put forward ideas of free will and personal responsibility?
7 What is the name given to the forward thinking movement of the fifteenth century?
8 In what way does Shakespeare use and reject the idea of courtly love in *Romeo and Juliet*?

Answers on p. 107.

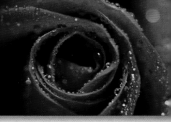

Plot and structure

Target your thinking

- What are the main events of the play? (**AO1**)
- How do these events unfold, scene by scene? (**AO1** and **AO2**)
- How does Shakespeare use structure in the telling of his tale? (**AO2**)

The events of the play span just five days. The first street fight takes place on a Sunday and the lovers have died by Thursday morning. Like all of Shakespeare's plays, *Romeo and Juliet* is divided into five acts. In Act 1, the main characters are presented and move the action of the play forward. The action rises in Act 2 and reaches a turning point in Act 3. An apparent solution is proposed in Act 4 and the consequences of this build the play's action to its dramatic conclusion in Act 5. Each act is also divided into scenes that take place in a certain location. Shakespeare's dramatic purpose is to present characters and events, stage by stage, so that the audience is carried along on the characters' journeys.

The Prologue

- We are told that the play is set in Verona.
- The events will be about two warring families of equal status.
- Romeo and Juliet are the doomed children of these families.
- The lovers' suicides will stop their parents from arguing.

The Prologue, in sonnet form, is used by Shakespeare to ensure that his audience knows the basic plot line *before* the play commences.

The Prologue is a literary device that was used in Greek tragedy. Typically, a group of minor characters from the play, called the Chorus, acted as a means of communicating directly to the audience, often commenting on what was happening on the stage and making some kind of moral evaluation of the characters' thoughts, feelings and actions. Shakespeare limits his use of the Chorus to this Prologue and one other intervention at the start of Act 2, but it is important to note that he is giving away the end of the play right at the outset. This is not usual practice in the telling of a story. He does not do it at the beginning of all his plays, which were also performed in the noisy Elizabethan theatres, so we must consider other reasons for why he does this. Shakespeare does not wish to reduce the tension of the play by telling us the story but rather to build anticipation for what is to come.

Key quotation

...*star-crossed lovers*...
(*Prologue 6*)

We learn that Romeo and Juliet are doomed to die. This introduces fate as one of the main themes of the play.

> **GRADE BOOSTER**
>
> ```
> To gain higher marks in the exam, you need to consider
> Shakespeare's use of form and structure - like the use
> of a Prologue - and how these inform the audience's
> understanding. The fact that Shakespeare gives away the
> ending at the beginning of the play could be seen as a
> suggestion to the audience that the real tragedy of this
> play is not in what happens, but in why it happens.
> ```

Act 1 overview: Sunday

- The Montague and Capulet servants fight.
- Romeo is lovesick for Rosaline.
- Paris asks Capulet if he can marry Juliet.
- Romeo, Benvolio and Mercutio go to the Capulets' ball.
- Tybalt wants to fight Romeo. Capulet prevents it.
- Romeo and Juliet meet and fall in love.

Act 1 scene 1

The scene opens with two Capulet servants boasting that they are far better than the Montagues. Two of Montague's servants appear and the Capulet servants taunt them, trying to start a fight. One 'bites' their thumb at the Montague servants, an insult expressing hatred and contempt.

Benvolio, from the house of Montague, tries to calm everyone down. Tybalt, one of the Capulets, insults the Montagues even more, enjoying the chance to fight them.

The Prince stops the fight and chastises both Capulet and Montague, threatening them with death should either of them disturb the peace again.

When the crowds have dispersed, the Montagues ask Benvolio if he has seen Romeo and the conversation turns to Romeo's recent depression. Benvolio tells them he will attempt to discover its cause. The two meet and we learn that Romeo is passionately in love with a girl called Rosaline who does not return his love. Romeo then notices signs of the fight and asks Benvolio what has happened, but then quickly adds, 'Yet tell me not, for I have heard it all', signalling that he is tired of all the fighting.

Key quotation

What, drawn and talk of peace? I hate the word, As I hate hell, all Montagues, and thee. Have at thee, coward. (1.1 61–63)

Build critical skills

Why do you think Shakespeare begins the play with a fight that escalates from a petty insult?

Build critical skills

Romeo says to Benvolio: 'Yet tell me not, for I have heard it all' and 'O any thing of nothing first create!' What point about the cause of the feud between the two households is Shakespeare reinforcing here through the character of Romeo?

Build critical skills

How does Shakespeare use the Capulet ball as a vehicle for the plot?

Build critical skills

In Elizabethan times, a father would choose a husband for his daughter and then inform her of his choice. What impression does Shakespeare give of Lord Capulet in his discussion with Paris?

Build critical skills

Shakespeare goes to great pains to point out to the audience just how deeply in love with Rosaline Romeo thinks he is. Why do you think Shakespeare does this so early on in the play?

Act 1 scene 2

Paris asks Capulet if he can marry his daughter, Juliet. At this early point in the play Capulet suggests that she is too young, having 'not seen the change of fourteen years'.

Paris points out that 'Younger than she are happy mothers made' and Capulet responds '...too soon marred are those so early made'.

Capulet sends off his servant with all the invitations to the party, but the servant can't read the names so Romeo reads them for him. Romeo discovers that Rosaline will be going to Capulet's party and Benvolio urges him to go as well so that he can prove that there are many more beautiful women than Rosaline.

Act 1 scene 3

Lady Capulet calls for her daughter, Juliet, before discussing with the Nurse how young she is. Lady Capulet asks Juliet what she thinks about getting married to Paris, saying many positive things about him. Juliet says she has not considered marriage yet but will be guided by her mother.

Act 1 scene 4

Romeo is reluctant to attend Capulet's party, having had a bad dream, but isn't given the opportunity to speak of it as Mercutio launches into a speech about dreams and 'Queen Mab', the fairy that races through the brains of those asleep and causes them to dream about specific things. His humorous tone changes though and becomes quite disturbed, as he transforms Queen Mab into a 'hag' and conjures degrading images of women.

Romeo appears concerned for his friend, telling him he talks of 'nothing', but then reveals his own bad feeling about going to the party. He is quite explicit here and suggests that he fears something will happen at this party over which he will have no control, but which will lead to his own 'untimely' (early) death.

▲ 'This night I hold an old accustomed feast.' (1.2 20)

Build critical skills

In scene 3, Juliet pledges allegiance to her mother's will but in scene 5 she spends time with Romeo without asking her mother's permission. This effect is called juxtapositioning. What effect is created by this juxtaposition?

Act 1 scene 5

Capulet gives a warm welcome to his guests. Romeo sees Juliet for the first time and falls instantly in love. Rosaline is forgotten, just as Benvolio predicted. Shakespeare even has Romeo use the same imagery that Benvolio used in Act 1 scene 2 when he said that another woman would make Romeo 'think thy swan a crow'. Romeo exclaims of Juliet 'So shows a snowy dove trooping with crows', meaning that other women are ugly crows compared to Juliet.

Tybalt hears Romeo and is determined to kill him for daring to come to their party. Capulet demands that Tybalt leaves Romeo alone, saying that Romeo is respected throughout Verona. Tybalt is not easily convinced until Capulet reminds him who is in charge, establishing his authority. Nevertheless, Shakespeare makes clear that Tybalt is storing up his anger for a later date.

Romeo approaches Juliet and touches her hand. The first fourteen lines of their dialogue forms a sonnet and presents the metaphor of Juliet as a holy shrine and Romeo as a pilgrim. The religious imagery here presents love as something spiritual. The lovers kiss. When Juliet is called away by the Nurse, Romeo discovers that Juliet is a Capulet and realises the serious consequences that will come from a relationship with her. As he leaves, Juliet questions the Nurse and learns Romeo's identity.

Build critical skills

What do the references to fate 'hanging in the stars' (1.5 107–109) and 'the steerage' (1.5 112–113) of the course of Romeo's life tell us about contemporary beliefs about destiny?

Key quotation

My only love sprung from my only hate! (1.5 137)

Juliet also says that she will die if she cannot marry Romeo. This comment proves ironic as she dies because she does marry him.

Act 2 overview: Sunday night and Monday morning

- The Prologue, in sonnet form, highlights how quickly the lovers' relationship is moving forward.
- Benvolio and Mercutio search for Romeo and fail to find him.
- Romeo secretly climbs into the Capulets' garden and sees Juliet at her window. They declare their love and plan to marry.
- The next morning, Romeo asks Friar Lawrence to marry him and Juliet.
- Tybalt sends Romeo a challenge to fight him.
- Romeo asks the Nurse to tell Juliet to meet him at the Friar's cell.
- Juliet arrives and the lovers leave with the Friar for a secret wedding.

Prologue to Act 2

The Prologue to Act 2 is in sonnet form, as it was at the start of the play. Sonnets were traditionally love poems, so this structure is appropriate in a play about love. This Prologue summarises what has happened so far so that events are made clear. It reminds us that Romeo has forgotten his love for Rosaline and that his relationship with Juliet is moving forward quickly. It is worth considering why Shakespeare uses the Chorus to tell the audience this, rather than one of the characters in the play. This could be because the Chorus is neither a friend nor enemy of the lovers, so presents an unbiased view of events.

Build critical skills

How does Shakespeare use personification in the first two lines of the Prologue to Act 2 to tell the audience about the strength of Romeo and Juliet's love?

Act 2 scene 1

Romeo doesn't want to leave the grounds of the house where Juliet is, so he stays and hides. His friends look for him, joking about his love for Rosaline. Mercutio again makes crude jokes where he talks of women as sexual objects. When Romeo won't come out from his hiding place, they go without him, but Mercutio is clearly disappointed.

Candidates who know the play well are able to make links between different aspects of the text. Such cross-referencing of events, characters and techniques will help you to gain marks. In Act 2 scene 1, for example, Mercutio uses crude language to describe what he thinks Romeo is doing with Rosaline. Find examples of Mercutio's language to contrast with examples of the pure language of love between Romeo and Juliet in Act 1 scene 5.

Act 2 scene 2

Romeo has overheard the conversation between Mercutio and Benvolio and states, 'He jests at scars that never felt a wound.'

This section is known as the 'balcony scene' although Shakespeare's stage directions mention a window rather than a balcony. Romeo speaks aloud to himself about Juliet's beauty, comparing her to light and brightness. Juliet speaks to the stars, while Romeo longs to be with her and to be able to touch her. Juliet expresses sadness that Romeo is a Montague because his name will cause problems. However, she states that if he won't deny his name, as long as he loves her, she will quite happily stop being a Capulet.

When Juliet tells Romeo that if he is found he will be killed, he tells her that he is more frightened of her rejection than of death. Juliet worries that having overheard her talk of her love for him, Romeo will think her too easily won and will not value her because of this. Romeo fears that it is all a dream: 'Too flattering-sweet to be substantial' (real). She tells him that if his love is 'honourable' and his 'purpose marriage', to send word to her the following day.

Build critical skills

What aspect of their love do you think Shakespeare wants his audience to consider? How might this quality of their relationship relate to what we have already been told will become of them?

The lovers are interrupted by the Nurse calling Juliet. They say a long goodbye with Juliet going and returning to the balcony. This emphasises their joy at being together and their reluctance to part.

Build critical skills

If Mercutio has 'never felt' the 'wound' of love, what does this suggest about his relationships with women?

Key quotation

What's in a name? That which we call a rose By any other word would smell as sweet; So Romeo would, were he not Romeo called... (2.2 43–45)

Build critical skills

How does Shakespeare build tension in this scene?

Key quotation

...Although I joy in thee, I have no joy of this contract tonight. It is too rash, too unadvised, too sudden... (2.2 116–118)

Key quotation

Parting is such sweet sorrow... (2.2 184)

Act 2 scene 3

Friar Lawrence looks out on the dawn rising and feels positive about the coming day, which is **ironic** considering later events. Shakespeare makes clear that the Friar has a good knowledge of herbs and potions. When Romeo arrives so early the Friar assumes he has been with Rosaline, thus we find out that Romeo confides more in the Friar than in his own parents who have earlier had to rely on Benvolio to try to find out why Romeo has been so out of spirits. When Romeo tells the Friar of his changed feelings, the Friar makes gentle fun of him for his sudden change of heart.

Nevertheless, the Friar agrees to help Romeo marry Juliet because he hopes their marriage will turn their households' 'rancour to pure love' and so end the feud between the Capulets and the Montagues, although he advises Romeo to take things slowly because rushing may result in problems. He warns 'they stumble that run fast'.

Act 2 scene 4

Mercutio and Benvolio are looking for Romeo, thinking he is still with Rosaline. Mercutio shows that his dislike of Rosaline stems from the alteration she has caused in Romeo's personality. They discuss a letter that Tybalt has sent, which challenges Romeo to a duel. Benvolio is certain Romeo will accept, but Mercutio suggests that he has been un-manned by Rosaline, 'stabbed with a white wench's black eye, run through the ear with a love-song…'. He questions, 'and is he a man to encounter Tybalt?' suggesting that Romeo is too love-struck to fight anyone. However, when Romeo appears, he seems back to his old self. He and Mercutio have a battle of wits.

The Nurse arrives and tells Romeo that she hopes his intentions are honourable. She is easily satisfied, though she does admit to having suggested to Juliet that Paris would be a better match for her. They arrange for Juliet to be at Friar Lawrence's cell that afternoon where he will marry them.

Act 2 scene 5

Juliet is impatiently waiting at home for the Nurse to return. She thinks the Nurse is too slow and speculates on the reasons why she has not come back, thinking perhaps she has not met Romeo. When she returns, the Nurse teases Juliet, praising Romeo's physical attractiveness, but making her wait for the news she wants to hear. At last she tells her of the plan, which Juliet receives with great joy.

Key quotation

Young men's love then lies
Not truly in their hearts, but in their eyes.
(2.3 67–68)

Build critical skills

Scene 3 is our first meeting with the Friar and Shakespeare takes care to signpost aspects of his character that will prove important later in the play. Why is it significant that he is collecting herbs when he is first introduced? What other aspects of his behaviour here suggest that he will be an important character in the play?

Build critical skills

Romeo stresses Rosaline's beauty many times in Act 1. Benvolio tells him to 'Examine other beauties'. Paris is described as a 'man of wax' (a perfect man like a sculptor's model) and Romeo is attracted to Juliet's 'true beauty'. What might Shakespeare be suggesting about attraction and love in the play?

Act 2 scene 6

The Friar asks heaven to bless the marriage and expresses his hopes that it won't lead to later regrets. Romeo doesn't care what may be in store, as long as he can call Juliet his wife. The Friar warns that intensity and fiery passion can burn out quickly and warns Romeo to 'love moderately' to ensure that he really knows what he's doing.

Once Juliet arrives, the Friar takes them to be married. The audience does not see the wedding between Romeo and Juliet. We are told it will be 'short work' (1.6 35) which suggests that Shakespeare wants the audience to focus on what happens after the ceremony rather than the marriage itself.

GRADE *BOOSTER*

```
Commenting on early events that foreshadow later ones
shows that you understand Shakespeare's structure and
how he lays the clues that confirm the tragic ending.
In Act 2 scene 6, the lovers are excited, passionate
and about to be married - in many ways, this is a happy
scene. However, re-read this short scene and you will
find clues that foreshadow the tragic end of the play.
```

Key quotation

These violent delights have violent ends.

(2.6 9)

Act 3 overview: Monday afternoon and Tuesday morning

- Tybalt kills Mercutio and Romeo kills Tybalt.
- The Prince banishes Romeo from Verona.
- Juliet hears of Tybalt's death and is distraught at Romeo's banishment.
- Romeo wants to kill himself but the Friar stops him.
- Capulet tells Paris that he can marry Juliet on Thursday.
- Romeo and Juliet spend Monday night together in secret.
- Juliet refuses to marry Paris.

Act 3 scene 1

Benvolio, the voice of reason, urges Mercutio to go inside and away from a potential brawl with the Capulets.

GRADE *BOOSTER*

```
Even if your exam question is about character rather
than theme, you will gain extra marks by showing how
characters and events support themes in the play.
This demonstrates to the examiner that you can see the
'bigger picture'. An ability to take an overview proves
that you understand how Shakespeare uses his characters
to put forward ideas in the play.
```

Key quotation

Ask for me tomorrow, and you shall find me a grave man.
(3.1 89)
A plague a'both your houses!
(3.1 97)

Mercutio challenges Tybalt. Romeo arrives and Tybalt calls him a 'villain' to provoke him but Romeo refuses to fight, saying, to Mercutio's amazement, that he 'loves' Tybalt, athough he can't explain why to him at the moment. This is because, by Romeo's secret marriage, Tybalt is now part of his family. Mercutio can't stand by and let Romeo disgrace himself by turning from a fight, so he fights Tybalt himself.

Romeo tries to calm the situation and stop the fighting but, by getting in the way, causes Mercutio to be fatally stabbed. Mercutio tries to laugh off his wounds in 'Ay, ay, a scratch, a scratch' (3.1 85) but he knows it is enough to kill him. He expresses his anger at the feud, which he sees as the cause of his untimely death.

Key quotation

O, I am fortune's fool.
(3.1 127)

Romeo vows to avenge Mercutio's death by killing Tybalt but as soon as he's done so, regards himself as the victim of fate.

Build critical skills

Note that Romeo blames fate for events but Mercutio blames the Capulets' and the Montagues' feud. See the section on 'Destiny' in *Context* on p. 12 for more on this. How does Shakespeare's inclusion of the contrasting ideas of fate and deliberate action reflect debates at the time?

Benvolio persuades Romeo to run away. The Prince arrives and Benvolio explains what has happened. Lady Capulet rushes in, sees Tybalt's body, and demands a revenge killing from the Prince. She accuses Benvolio of lying, showing how close she was to Tybalt. Montague reminds the Prince that in killing Tybalt, Romeo has merely brought about what the law would have demanded anyway – Tybalt's life for killing Mercutio. It is also revealed that Mercutio was the Prince's own kinsman (relative). As a compromise, Romeo is banished but had better go 'in haste', or he will be killed.

Build critical skills

Keep in mind how Shakespeare has constructed the play for maximum excitement and tension. At the end of scene 1, for example, Romeo is not served the death penalty but is banished. This is a plot device. Why do you think Shakespeare has opted to use this as a punishment?

Act 3 scene 2

Juliet is anticipating spending the night with Romeo, when the Nurse arrives with news of the fight, making it sound as if Romeo is dead. When Juliet discovers the truth, she feels betrayed by Romeo.

When Juliet has reconciled herself to the death of her cousin, realising that Tybalt would have killed Romeo if Romeo had not killed him, she mourns the fact that she and Romeo will now not have a wedding night. She pledges to die a virgin and seems intent on killing herself, commenting that 'death, not Romeo, take my maidenhead!' To comfort her, the Nurse offers to fetch Romeo and bring him secretly to Juliet's bedroom. The Nurse is Juliet's trusted confidante here, which is why it is surprising when the Nurse lets her down at the end of this act.

GRADE BOOSTER

Candidates who are able to take an overview and cross-reference aspects of the play will be awarded higher marks. In Juliet's first soliloquy in this scene, she speaks of Romeo as if he is a light that can be cut out 'in little stars' if she dies. Refer to the first Prologue to find similar use of imagery. What themes are being presented here?

Act 3 scene 3

The Friar tries to see the positive side of Romeo's situation, saying 'the world is broad and wide', but Romeo sees his banishment as a form of death as he will be separated from Juliet. The Friar is annoyed that Romeo is ungrateful that his life has been saved. This fails to convince Romeo, who sees it as 'torture' because Verona is 'heaven' as it is 'where Juliet lives' (3.3 30).

The Nurse arrives on an 'errand' from Juliet. She sees Romeo crying and criticises his behaviour, demanding, 'Stand up, stand up, stand, and you be a man.' (3.3 88) Romeo is worried that Juliet despises him for being an 'old murderer' and attempts to kill himself. The Friar prevents him.

Key quotation

O serpent heart, hid with a flow'ring face! Did ever dragon keep so fair a cave? Beautiful tyrant, fiend angelical!
(3.2 73–75)

Build critical skills

How does Shakespeare use contrasting emotions and dramatic irony in Act 3 scene 2?

Build critical skills

Romeo behaves very emotionally and dramatically in scene 3. How is this consistent with what we have seen of Romeo's behaviour elsewhere in the play?

Key quotation

Art thou a man? Thy form cried out thou art; Thy tears are womanish, thy wild acts denote The unreasonable fury of a beast.
(3.3 108–110)

25

The Friar feels responsible for the way events have turned out and tries to rectify them by sending Romeo to Juliet briefly, planning for Romeo to then travel to Mantua and wait there until the Friar can find a way of publicising their marriage and reconciling the families.

Act 3 scene 4

Capulet tells Paris that he has not been able to talk to Juliet about a potential marriage because she is mourning the death of her cousin. He then reconsiders his delay and abandons his earlier leniency, saying Juliet will marry Paris. His belief that she will readily agree to her father's choice is ironic.

Although it is the early hours of the morning, he instructs Lady Capulet to go and see Juliet before going to bed, to tell her about the intended marriage to Paris.

▲ Leonardo DiCaprio as Romeo and Claire Danes as Juliet in the 1996 Luhrmann adaptation

Act 3 scene 5

The lovers' parting is a sensitive and poignant part of the play. After just one night, they must now separate. Juliet begs Romeo to stay, claiming they heard a nightingale singing, not the morning lark, but Romeo assures her it is morning and he must leave quickly for Mantua. The Nurse arrives to warn Juliet that her mother is on her way and that they must 'be wary'. As Romeo climbs from Juliet's window, she looks down on him, foreshadowing the play's ending.

Lady Capulet arrives and tells Juliet that she must not mourn Tybalt's death too much and needs to control herself. This scene is very ironic as Juliet is actually crying because Romeo has left, whilst Lady Capulet vows vengeance on Romeo for killing Tybalt and assumes that Juliet agrees with her plans. There is further irony in the fact that Lady Capulet plans for Romeo to be poisoned, and in Act 5 Romeo voluntarily drinks a poison. Lady Capulet reveals the details of the planned wedding to Paris. Juliet refuses. Capulet enters, expecting Juliet to be happy about the news. He is initially sympathetic about her supposed grief for Tybalt but soon becomes enraged at her refusal to marry. He threatens to throw her out of the house if she doesn't change her mind.

Here, 'and' means 'if'. Capulet is saying that either Juliet accepts that she is his possession that he can give to whomever he wishes, or she can leave. Remember that the play is set in fourteenth-century Italy. Arranged marriages were common. As an unmarried woman, not brought up to work, Juliet would be unable to support herself. She cannot run away and is effectively now trapped.

Juliet appeals first to her mother, who shows no sympathy at all, then to her trusted Nurse for consolation. Surprisingly, the Nurse advises 'I think it best you married with the County' and Juliet realises that she is truly alone. She shows strength of character here in now hiding her feelings from the Nurse and claiming she wishes to confess her sinful refusal to the Friar. Once the Nurse has gone, Juliet reveals her true plans and feelings in her soliloquy. She accepts that she must find a solution outside the family and vows that if the Friar cannot help her, she will kill herself.

Act 4 overview: Tuesday day and Wednesday morning

- The Friar gives Juliet a potion that will make her temporarily 'dead'.
- They plan Juliet's eventual escape to Mantua.
- Juliet returns home. She lies and tells her father that she will marry Paris.
- The marriage is brought forward to Wednesday.
- Juliet takes the drug on Tuesday night.

Key quotation

Methinks I see thee now, thou art so low, As one dead in the bottom of a tomb.
(3.5 55–56)

Key quotation

And you be mine, I'll give you to my friend; And you be not, hang, beg, starve, die in the streets.
(3.5 191–192)

Build critical skills

How do Capulet's words and actions give us an insight into why there are problems between the Capulets and the Montagues?

Build critical skills

Use your skills of overview! Contrast Juliet's feelings at the start of scene 5 with her feelings at the end.

27

- On Wednesday morning, the Nurse finds Juliet, apparently dead.
- The Friar tells the Capulets to bring Juliet for burial.

Act 4 scene 1

Paris is visiting Friar Lawrence to tell him about his plans to marry Juliet. The Friar is understandably surprised and tells him 'the time is very short' but Paris explains that it is to help Juliet to overcome her grief at Tybalt's death. Juliet arrives. Paris greets her as his 'lady' and his 'wife' and she responds fairly coldly to him and with answers that have a double meaning. The audience understands the true meaning of her responses but Paris does not.

> **GRADE BOOSTER**
>
> Look for opportunities to embed context into your argument. In this scene, Paris says to Juliet, 'Thy face is mine' and regards her as his possession, just as her father does. Consider what comment Shakespeare might be making about oppressive male attitudes towards women.

Key quotation

O bid me leap, rather than marry Paris, From off the battlements of any tower.
(4.1 77–78)

When Paris leaves, the Friar initially states that he knows of no remedy to her plight. However, when Juliet threatens suicide, he says that he can 'spy a kind of hope' and proposes a potion that will make Juliet appear dead for forty-two hours. The Friar instructs Juliet to go home and pretend to give consent to marry Paris. She is to take the drug at night, then will be found in the morning and taken to the Capulets' burial vault. The Friar will send a letter to Mantua to tell Romeo of the plan so that he will be by Juliet's side when she wakes. Here, we see Juliet's true resolve and strength of character. She is willing to die to avoid marrying Paris and risks death by taking a dangerous drug.

> **GRADE BOOSTER**
>
> Remember that paying attention to the craft of the writer will gain you marks in AO2. The audience already knows that Romeo and Juliet will die as this was stated in the Prologue. However, the idea of the Friar 'spy[ing] a kind of hope' raises the audience's expectations that the lovers' may still escape their fate. In this way, Shakespeare maintains tension in the play.

Act 4 scene 2

Though short, this scene is filled with irony. Capulet is forging ahead with the marriage plans when Juliet returns from the Friar and pleads for forgiveness for her behaviour, saying that she repents her 'disobedient opposition' (4.2 17). Despite her secret plans for that evening, she tells her father that 'Henceforward I am ever ruled by you.' (4.2 21) We know that, as the play has progressed, Juliet has learnt to evade her father's 'behests' (wishes) and to follow her own course. She uses the art of subterfuge (being deceptive) in order to do this.

In another clever move, Juliet purposely asks the Nurse to help her pick out some clothes to 'furnish (her) tomorrow', yet the wedding is meant to be in two days – Thursday – not the very next day. Juliet is implying that she is ready to marry. This is a double ruse (trick). Firstly, her father will think that she is eager to marry Paris. Secondly, she can carry out her plan of taking the drug that night and so – as she thinks – be reunited with Romeo much more quickly. Indeed, her father seizes on the subtle suggestion and asserts 'we'll to church tomorrow'. There is also irony in Capulet's fervent praise of the 'reverend holy Friar' who, of course, has helped Juliet to plot against her father.

Act 4 scene 3

Juliet asks the Nurse to leave her alone for the night, telling her she has to pray. Alone, Juliet speculates as to whether the potion will work or if it might be a deadly poison that the Friar has given to her to save himself from the dishonour of having to marry her to Paris when he has already married her to someone else. Her doubts about the Friar's motives are particularly pertinent when we see his actions at the end of the play. Juliet's imagination also conjures frightening ideas of her revival in the tomb and she fears waking before Romeo arrives, being suffocated, seeing ghosts and going mad.

Nevertheless, she takes the potion, with the words, 'Romeo, Romeo, Romeo! Here's drink – I drink to thee.' (4.3 58) Ironically, when Juliet does wake, the sight she is met with is worse than any she envisaged.

Shakespeare's clever crafting of the play is in evidence in this scene. By having Juliet effectively say her last farewell to the world at this stage, Shakespeare is able to then pick up the pace at the play's **denouement** when Juliet actually dies. A lengthy speech at the play's end would reduce the tension.

Act 4 scene 4

As the wedding preparations continue, Capulet urges everyone to hurry up. He is excited and in a positive frame of mind. There is irony in this scene as the audience knows that Juliet lies apparently 'dead', whilst these futile wedding preparations are going on in another room.

Build critical skills

Note how Shakespeare makes his characters convincing by giving them a variety of personality traits. Capulet seemed a tolerant father at the outset, proposing that any suitor for Juliet must meet with her approval. Later, his rage at her refusal to marry presents him as a cruel person. How do you respond to his behaviour in Act 4 scene 2?

denouement: the ending of a plot or story, where the outcome is explained.

Key quotation

Death lies upon her like an untimely frost Upon the sweetest flower of all the field. (4.5 28–29)

Build critical skills

The frequent references to death remind us that it is both a significant theme and motif in the play. Shakespeare personifies Death when he has Capulet exclaim:

Death is my son-in-law, Death is my heir,

My daughter he hath wedded…

(4.5 38–39)

Think about the ending of the play. Why are Capulet's words so poignant?

Act 4 scene 5

The Nurse initially believes that Juliet is being lazy. Discovering that she is actually 'dead', she calls Juliet's parents who are distraught. Their words are poetic.

GRADE BOOSTER

Candidates who are able to consider different interpretations will offer judgements about characters and events rather than merely coming to definite conclusions. This 'informed personal response' to the play will be awarded higher marks. Here, the family's mourning can be seen to be filled with anguish or, alternatively, regarded as a little absurd, particularly in the Nurse's lines.

Capulet and his wife seemed to present a united front through the play, both agreeing that Juliet should marry Paris. However, there have been clues of underlying tensions, such as Lady Capulet declaring her husband 'too hot' (mad) in his earlier rage against Juliet. Now, at Juliet's death, Lady Capulet declares her the 'one thing' she had 'to rejoice and solace in', hinting further at an unhappy marriage.

The Friar tells the Capulets to prepare to follow the body of Juliet to her grave. He urges them to refrain from over-indulgent mourning because it will irritate heaven.

Act 5 overview: Wednesday day and Thursday morning

- Romeo hears of Juliet's death and leaves for Verona.
- Paris and Romeo fight at the tomb. Romeo kills Paris.
- Romeo kisses Juliet, then poisons himself.
- Juliet wakes, finds Romeo dead and stabs herself.
- The Montagues and Capulets make peace with each other.

Act 5 scene 1

Romeo is lonely in Mantua. He recounts a dream where Juliet finds him dead but revives him with a kiss. His dream in Act 1, although not explained, filled him with foreboding and dark thoughts. These dreams suggest he senses his untimely death. His servant, Balthasar, then arrives from Verona with news of Juliet's death. As in Act 3, when he killed Mercutio, Romeo feels that the fates are against him.

Key quotation

I defy you, stars! (5.1 24)

Romeo has not received the Friar's intended letter, explaining that Juliet is drugged, not dead. The fact that the message never arrived is yet another misfortune to happen to Romeo and Juliet in the play.

Romeo, devastated by the news, prepares to return to be with Juliet's body. As previously in the play, he acts on impulse and does not consider that the wise thing to do would be to talk to the Friar before taking further action. Romeo dismisses Balthasar hastily and makes a quick decision to visit an apothecary he has already noticed in Mantua. He demands 'A dram of poison' and the apothecary agrees because he is poor and desperate for money.

> **GRADE** *BOOSTER*
>
> You will gain marks by showing an understanding of Shakespeare's careful structure. In Act 5, Romeo first sees the apothecary 'culling of simples' (picking herbs for medicine), echoing the Friar's first introduction in Act 2 when he was also seen gathering plants. The Friar speaks of those who 'misappl[y]' and 'abuse' their knowledge of 'plants, herbs, stones' which is duly shown in the apothecary's willingness to supply Romeo with a deadly drug. There is a further link to Lady Capulet's wish in Act 3 that an 'unaccustomed dram' will kill Romeo. Note that these clever cross-references display Shakespeare's precise structure.

Build critical skills

Make a list of all the things that happen to Romeo and Juliet in the play that could be called unlucky. In each case, consider whether these events could be explained as the result of human causes.

Act 5 scene 2

Friar Lawrence asks Friar John whether he has a message or a letter for him from Romeo. Friar John tells him that he has been unable to see Romeo because he was prevented from going to Mantua. The Friar curses fortune, as the letter contained details of his plan.

The Friar decides to take dramatic action to prevent disaster. He resolves to be at the tomb when Juliet awakes and vows to write again to Mantua, so that Romeo will know what has happened. He will keep Juliet at his place, hidden, until Romeo returns for her.

Act 5 scene 3

Paris, grief stricken, has gone to mourn his loss outside the tomb where Juliet lies. Romeo arrives with Balthasar and gives his servant a letter to take to his father. He tells Balthasar to leave, but he hides instead and witnesses Romeo breaking open Juliet's tomb. Shakespeare has Romeo personify the earth as a pregnant woman, whose womb holds not life, but death.

Key quotation

Thou detestable maw, thou womb of death, Gorged with the dearest morsel of the earth...
(5.3 45–46)

Key quotation

...O true apothecary!
Thy drugs are quick.
Thus with a kiss I die.
(5.3 119–120)

Paris challenges Romeo, thinking he has come to do something terrible to the dead bodies. He calls him 'vile Montague!' (5.3 54) reminding the audience of the feud. Romeo's impetuous fight with Tybalt is echoed here, as Romeo challenges Paris and kills him. Romeo is filled with remorse, showing his compassionate nature. As a tribute, he places Paris by Juliet. Romeo's farewell speech to Juliet is reminiscent of her words before taking the sleeping drug in Act 4. Romeo takes the poison, which has an immediate effect.

▲ Juliet's 'deathbed' in the 1996 Luhrmann adaptation

Build critical skills

The deaths of Romeo and Juliet are at the centre of this scene, but Shakespeare also uses them to add depth to other characters. How are Paris and the Friar presented in the scene?

At this exact moment Friar Lawrence arrives, enters the tomb and, finding Romeo and Paris dead, curses time and fate that allowed this to happen. Juliet wakes, but before the Friar can relate the terrible events they hear a noise and he urges her to come with him. Juliet, seeing Romeo, refuses to leave. The Friar is hasty in abandoning her and fears, 'I dare no longer stay' (5.3 159).

Juliet guesses how Romeo has died and kisses him in the hope that there is sufficient poison on his lips to kill her. When this fails, she kills herself with his dagger, falling on his body.

Balthasar and the Friar are captured as the Prince, Capulet and Lady Capulet arrive. Montague brings news that his wife has died due to the shock of Romeo's exile. The Friar relates a lengthy account of events, although it seems he is doing it to plead his innocence. A letter that Romeo has left for his father corroborates the Friar's story. The Prince condemns the families' conflict and observes that 'All are punished' meaning that they have now paid bitterly for their quarrel. The families reconcile. Montague tells Capulet he will commission a gold statue of Juliet and Capulet promises one of Romeo. The lovers will be immortalised as a symbol of true love.

In Shakespearean tradition, the highest-ranking character has the final words. Here, the Prince reflects on events. The Prologue foretold that the 'parents' strife' would be buried by the play's denouement. Truly, through Romeo and Juliet's deaths, love has conquered all.

Timeline

Events in the play take place over just four days.

SUNDAY	
Act 1 scene 1	Street brawl – Sunday 9 a.m. It is 'new struck nine' (1.1 152)
Act 1 scene 5	Capulet's party – Sunday evening
MONDAY	
Act 2 scenes 1–3	Sunday night to Monday morning Romeo outside Juliet's bedroom The Friar watching dawn in his cell
Act 2 scene 6	Romeo and Juliet marry – Monday afternoon
Act 3 scene 1	Later Monday afternoon – Mercutio fights with Tybalt
Act 3 scene 4	Late Monday night – Romeo and Juliet are together
TUESDAY	
Act 3 scene 5	Tuesday dawn – Romeo leaves and immediately afterwards Juliet's mother, who has not yet been to bed, informs her of the planned wedding between her and Paris
Act 4 scene 2	Juliet's marriage is brought forward from Thursday to Wednesday
Act 4 scene 3	Juliet takes the potion
WEDNESDAY	
Act 4 scene 5	Wednesday morning – Juliet is found 'dead'
Act 5 scene 1	Wednesday day – Romeo leaves Mantua to return to Verona Wednesday evening/night – Romeo arrives at Juliet's grave, fights Paris and kills himself. Juliet wakes and kills herself
THURSDAY	
Act 5 scene 3	Dawn breaks on Thursday morning as the Prince sums up events

The structure of the play

The Prologue introduces us to life in Verona and gives an overview of events, inviting us into 'the two hour's traffic of [the] stage'. By establishing the play's tragic ending from the outset, Shakespeare seems to be attributing coming events to an inescapable fate. Duly, by the play's denouement, the action outlined in the Prologue has taken place. The lovers die and 'their death' ends their 'parents' strife'. The opening and closing lines of the play are thereby linked.

Another way of looking at the structure is to consider it in terms of exposition, rising action, climax and denouement. Act 1 provides the exposition, where the action is quickly established with the first fight scene, which clearly establishes the impact that the families' feud has on life in Verona.

The instigator in events is Romeo, who sets events in motion by declaring his immediate attraction to Juliet. The rising action occurs in the exchange of the lovers' vows in the balcony scene. Their marriage leads from this, which prevents Romeo from wanting to fight his 'relative' Tybalt, resulting in Mercutio's death, Tybalt's death and, ultimately, Romeo's banishment. The climax of the play is hastened by Capulet's decision to marry Juliet to Paris. From this, Juliet fakes her own death which in turn leads to Romeo's suicide and then her own. The denouement comes in the discovery of the bodies and the final reconciliation of the families.

GRADE *FOCUS*

Grade 5

Students will be able to show a clear and detailed understanding of the whole text and of the effects created by its structure.

Grade 8

Students' responses will display a comprehensive understanding of explicit and implicit meanings in the text as a whole and will examine and evaluate the writer's use of structure in detail.

REVIEW YOUR LEARNING

1 How does the Prologue describe the lovers?

2 Why doesn't Romeo want to hear the cause of the fight in Act 1?

3 How are Juliet's parents presented in Act 1 of the play?

4 In what ways is Mercutio's personality different from Romeo's? In what ways is it similar?

5 What does the Prologue to Act 2 tell us about Romeo and Juliet's relationship?

6 What reservations does Juliet have about the speed at which her and Romeo's relationship is developing?

7 How are Juliet's parents presented in Act 3 of the play?

8 The Friar abandons Juliet in the play's final scene. Can you find any clues earlier in the play that he was quite a hasty person?

9 Who speaks the final words of the play?

10 In what way might the play be described as cyclical in structure?

Answers on p. 107.

Characterisation

Target your thinking

- Who are the main protagonists in the play? (**AO1**)
- How does Shakespeare make his characters come to life? (**AO2**)
- What purposes are served by the characters? (**AO1** and **AO2**)
- Do the characters have symbolic value? (**AO1**, **AO2** and **AO3**)

Romeo

Shakespeare presents Romeo as the archetypal young lover. He is emotional and often impulsive. The first time we meet him, he is depressed, bemoaning, 'Ay me, sad hours seem long' (1.1 152).

▲ Leonardo DiCaprio as Romeo in the Luhrmann film

According to his friends, Romeo has been acting out of character. The woman he loves, Rosaline, does not love him. When he is happily in love with Juliet in Act 2, he becomes more quick-witted and humorous. Shakespeare emphasises Romeo's tendency to react emotionally to events. When the others are excited about Capulet's party, Romeo is presented as withdrawn:

> ...I have a soul of lead
>
> So stakes me to the ground I cannot move.
>
> (1.4 15–16)

GRADE BOOSTER

Even if your exam question asks you to look at how a character is presented, you also need to consider how they illustrate certain themes. This demonstrates that you understand Shakespeare's craft and how he uses characters to present themes.

Key quotation

Did my heart love till now? Foreswear it, sight! For I ne'er saw true beauty till this night.
(1.5 51–52)

When Romeo sees Juliet for the first time he is shown to be mesmerised by her, exclaiming, 'O she doth teach the torches to burn bright!' which seems fickle after his depression over Rosaline. This swift transfer of affections might lead an audience to wonder if this is love or infatuation.

Shakespeare highlights a variety of personality traits in Romeo. He is shown to be respected around Verona when Capulet notes that Romeo is 'a virtuous and well-governed youth' (1.5 66–67) but he is also presented as making reckless decisions, such as risking his life by climbing into the Capulet's garden to see Juliet. He is shown to be calm when confronted with violence in Act 3 scene 1 as he tries to diffuse the situation. Unfortunately, his attempts to stop the fight result in Mercutio's death as he gets in the way. He then switches quickly to violence, killing Tybalt swiftly.

Build critical skills

Consider in what ways Romeo's behaviour leads to many of the key events in the play. How far does Shakespeare present him as accepting responsibility for his actions?

Shakespeare highlights Romeo's refusal to see reason when he reacts in an extreme manner to his banishment, telling the Friar that it is a 'torture' worse than death, throwing himself on the floor crying and then trying to stab himself. Similarly, in Act 5 when he discovers Juliet is dead he rushes to an apothecary to buy poison, then back to Verona to kill himself by her side. A little more patience and an attempt to communicate with the Friar could have resulted in a happy ending.

Juliet

Juliet's character changes gradually throughout the play. Initially, Shakespeare portrays her as an innocent girl whom her father, Capulet, is protective of as she is only 13 years old.

Key quotation

My child is yet a stranger in the world, She hath not seen the change of fourteen years;
(1.2 8–9)

▲ Claire Danes as Juliet in the Luhrmann film

Juliet is presented as obedient to her mother in her first scene when she says: 'Madam, I am here. What is your will?' (1.3 7) She is described by the Nurse as 'the prettiest babe that e'er I nursed' (1.3 61), creating the idea of Juliet's beauty and preparing the audience for Romeo's reaction to her.

Although she appears to be subservient to her parents, Shakespeare highlights that she does not instantly agree to marry Paris but says that she'll try to like him, 'if looking liking move' (1.3 98). Notice the difference in her passionate attraction to Romeo.

Shakespeare presents Juliet as more level-headed than Romeo. In Act 2 scene 2, she expresses concern that their relationship is 'rash' and 'unadvis'd'. Shakespeare shows Juliet to be a convincing mix of teenage enthusiasm and mature consideration. We are reminded of her young age in Act 2 scene 5 in her impatience and excitement when waiting for the Nurse's message from Romeo.

Her self-confidence grows as the play progresses and she tries to direct the course of her own life. She is adamant that she will not marry Paris, although societal expectations at the time would have expected **filial** obedience.

filial: relating to a son or daughter.

Key quotation

*O sweet my mother,
cast me not away!
Delay this marriage for
a month, a week...
(3.5 198–199)*

In Juliet, Shakespeare has created a character who is quite manipulative, seen when trying to persuade Romeo to stay longer in Act 3 scene 5, the way she tries to play off her mother and father against each other in Act 3 scene 5, and when she lies to her father that she has repented 'the sin of disobedient opposition' in Act 4 scene 2.

Shakespeare has Juliet use clever dialogue when speaking to Paris. The quick-fire language of Act 4 scene 1 shows that while Juliet does not criticise Paris openly, she is hinting at the fact that she does not love him.

GRADE *BOOSTER*

> The presentation of Juliet could reveal Shakespeare's disapproval of a society in which the repression of women means that they are driven to deception. Speculation of possible authorial intention will help to boost your grade.

GRADE *BOOSTER*

> Always write about the characters as Shakespeare's inventions rather than real people. Juliet is obviously not a real person but a character that Shakespeare has created.

Juliet's beauty is repeatedly stressed in the play, even when apparently dead. Romeo comments ironically that she almost looks alive as there is 'crimson' in her cheeks and little evidence of 'death's pale flag' (5.3 95–96).

Shakespeare presents Juliet's suicide as a quick, impulsive act but also as a courageous one. She is a character who resists what is expected of a 13-year-old girl of this time, determined to be with the man she wants, in life or death.

Mercutio

Mercutio is a kinsman to the Prince and Romeo's good friend. He is presented as passionate, clever and courageous and with a highly developed sense of honour. Shakespeare gives Mercutio explicit language, full of wordplay and sexual double entendres. Rejecting the idea of romantic love, Mercutio mocks Romeo's lovesick behaviour. He dismisses dreams as idle fantasies in order to show Romeo that his attraction to Rosaline is a passing fancy.

Shakespeare also highlights Mercutio's interest in Romeo. In the scenes where Mercutio appears, the conversation revolves around his friend: where he is, what he's doing, his emotional or mental state.

When Romeo disappears after the feast, Shakespeare has Mercutio try to tease him out of hiding, telling him to 'cry but "Ay me"' or 'love' or 'dove', showing that Mercutio believes Romeo has been made effeminate through love of women. Romeo's response to this, 'he jests at scars that never felt a wound', confirms to the audience that Mercutio has never been in love.

Shakespeare shows Romeo to be sometimes irritated by Mercutio, exclaiming 'Peace, peace, Mercutio, peace!/Thou talk'st of nothing' (1.4 95–96) and calling him someone who 'loves to hear himself talk' (2.4 123) but Romeo also jokes with Mercutio and enjoys their battles of wit. Mercutio's wild words also lead him to be rude to the Nurse and speak insultingly of women, calling 'Dido a dowdy, Cleopatra a gypsy, Helen and Hero/hildings and harlots…'.

Mercutio is presented as loyal to his friends in fearing that Romeo's obsession with Rosaline means that he is not fit to confront Tybalt's challenge. Instead, Mercutio is spoiling for a fight himself. Shakespeare highlights his agitation by presenting his speeches in prose here and not verse, as with his earlier speeches regarding the absence of Romeo.

Mercutio is presented as horrified by Romeo's attempts to pacify Tybalt. In society at this time, it was seen as unmanly to tolerate an insult. Mercutio therefore regards Romeo's submission as 'vile' and 'dishonourable' and steps in to protect Romeo.

In his dying moments, the repetition of 'A plague a' both your houses!' (3.1 83 and 97) emphasises his belief that the feud has caused his death.

Mercutio is certainly entertaining, but he is also a plot device. He encourages Romeo to attend the Capulets' ball and his death results in Romeo killing Tybalt and being banished, which sets in motion later events. He illustrates the themes of friendship and conflict. His coarse language presents a different view of women and love to that which Romeo holds, allowing us to see what a romantic Romeo is. Also, by removing him from the play quite early on, Shakespeare encourages us to focus on the tragedy of the two main protagonists.

> **Build critical skills**
>
> Mercutio blames the Montagues and the Capulets for his death. Consider whether Mercutio's death is entirely the result of the feud, or whether his actions cause his own downfall.

Nurse

Shakespeare presents the Nurse as Juliet's protector and helper and she is far closer to Juliet than her mother is. She even breast-fed Juliet as a baby, which was not at all unusual at the time. The Nurse is often a comic character. Shakespeare infuses her speeches with sexual innuendo, reflected in the eagerness with which the Nurse is complicit in arranging Juliet's marriage to Romeo. Shakespeare reveals her to be irresponsible.

Following Juliet's marriage to Romeo and after the death of Tybalt, Shakespeare has the Nurse continue to help Juliet as much as she can, highlighting that she wishes Juliet to be happy. In Act 3 scene 2 she offers Juliet hope by saying that she will bring Romeo to comfort Juliet. The Nurse also brings warning of Lady Capulet's approach when Juliet is with Romeo and leaps to her defence when Capulet is enraged by Juliet's refusal to marry Paris.

> **Key quotation**
>
> *I am the drudge and toil in your delight;*
> *But you shall bear the burden soon at night.*
> *(2.5 74–75)*

Build critical skills

The Nurse is perfectly happy for Juliet to marry Paris. Through the Nurse's casual acceptance of Juliet's sudden second match, what point might Shakespeare be making about attitudes towards marriage in this period?

However, Shakespeare has the Nurse draw the line at outright defiance of Lord Capulet's commands, saying 'I think you had better marry with the County' and she tries to reconcile Juliet to the arrangement by telling her that Paris is a better match.

Shakespeare shows her to be totally unabashed in suggesting that Juliet coolly transfer her affections to Paris. For the Nurse, the critical factor is that Juliet will not be found out, telling her, '...here it is:/Romeo is banished ... he dares ne'er come back to challenge you' (3.5 212–214). This shows that male oppression has led her to feel no guilt at all in using deceit to cover her tracks. Shakespeare shows that she believes one man is as good as another provided they are good-looking and have lots of money.

Juliet later sees the Nurse as a false friend, calling her, 'Ancient damnation! O most wicked fiend!' for formerly praising Romeo and now insulting him. Shakespeare does not have Juliet confide in the Nurse after this point. It is fitting that it is the Nurse who finds Juliet supposedly dead in Act 4 scene 4. Until the Nurse's support of Capulet's plans, she was always Juliet's confidante and had true affection for her. She is devastated by Juliet's death.

Friar Lawrence

Friar Lawrence's role as a man with knowledge of drugs, medicines and potions is established from the outset when Shakespeare gives him the lines:

> O mickle is the powerful grace that lies
>
> In herbs, plants, stones, and their true qualities…
>
> (2.3 15–16)

Here he muses over the power of herbs to do both good and bad, linking to the Friar's own power to influence events. Romeo calls him 'my ghostly father' (2.3 45) and 'ghostly sire' (2.2 188), and Juliet adds, 'my ghostly confessor' (2.6 21). In these words, Shakespeare lends a sense of mystery and authority to the character and he reinforces this through often presenting the Friar alone.

The Friar is cross at Romeo's rapid change of affections. He urges Romeo to be less hasty, upbraiding him for his fickle nature and reminding him that he was only recently crying over Rosaline.

Despite this, he agrees to help Romeo because he hopes the lovers' marriage will end the feud between the two families, commenting that the alliance might 'turn your households' rancour to pure love'. However, he still preaches wariness to Romeo, warning him that 'they stumble that run fast' and 'violent delights have violent ends'.

Key quotation

Young men's love then lies Not truly in their hearts, but in their eyes (2.3 67–68)

The Friar is a plot device: marrying the lovers, suggesting that Romeo sneak into Juliet's room for their wedding night, arranging for passage to Mantua and devising the plan to reunite the lovers. Yet, despite this input, Shakespeare draws attention to the Friar's tendency to blame events on outside forces and highlights his refusal to accept any responsibility for events. Instead, the Friar curses time and fate that have allowed events to happen.

The Friar's role at the end of the play is to summarise events for the Prince, and for the audience too. He states at the end that, 'if ought in this/Miscarried by my fault, let my old life/Be sacrificed...', suggesting that he is willing to die if he has been in any way at fault. Yet this could be interpreted as an over-dramatic plea because he knows that society trusts him. Indeed, the Prince immediately comments, 'We still have known thee for a holy man.'

Ultimately, the Friar has good motives but his decisions play a considerable part in the tragic outcome.

> **Key quotation**
>
> *...Ah, what an unkind hour*
> *Is guilty of this lamentable chance!*
> *(5.3 145–146)*

GRADE *BOOSTER*

Candidates who explore Shakespeare's presentation of the complex nature of the Friar, rather than decide if he is definitively good or bad, will achieve higher marks. He is not one-dimensional but has his good points and his failings. He may be a priest, but he is also portrayed as very human. Make sure you are aware of his good points and his failings.

Benvolio

Shakespeare presents Benvolio as a peacemaker and a figure of calm common sense throughout the play. His opening words are an attempt to stop the first fight in the play and he resists Tybalt's challenge to join in, explaining, 'I do but keep the peace...' (1.1 59).

Benvolio is a good friend to Romeo and Mercutio and advises both of them to be calm. As Romeo's confidant, he tries to cheer him up, encouraging him to attend the Capulets' ball and 'Examine other beauties' (1.1 219). He is a calming influence, but it is interesting that Mercutio speaks of Benvolio's short temper in Act 3 scene 1, saying that he has seen Benvolio quarrel 'with a man for coughing in the street' (line 21). However, knowing Mercutio's teasing manner, it is more likely that Mercutio is describing himself and attributing it to Benvolio in the hope that he'll join in with fighting the Capulets. Shakespeare gives Benvolio narratives that summarise events. Lady Capulet doubts his sincerity, but his accounts are true reflections of events.

> **Key quotation**
>
> *This is the truth, or let Benvolio die.*
> *(3.1 166)*

Tybalt

Tybalt, Juliet's cousin, speaks only thirty-six lines in the play yet behaves aggressively in every scene he appears in. In Act 1 scene 1 he threatens one of the play's most honest characters when he says, 'Turn thee, Benvolio, look upon thy death.' (line 58)

Tybalt enjoys the opportunity to fight and answers Benvolio's plea for help in stopping the fight with yet another challenge.

When Benvolio discusses Tybalt with Montague, he gives an honest assessment of his character, calling him 'fiery' and having 'defiance'.

Build critical skills

There are many references to daggers and weapons in the play. Find five references and comment on their effect.

At Capulet's party in Act 1 scene 5, Tybalt sees Romeo's presence as an insult and a challenge to the family honour. Tybalt challenges Capulet's request for restraint, sneering, 'I'll not endure him' (1.5 75) and thereby inciting Capulet's rage. Capulet calls him 'goodman boy' (someone who is not a gentleman), 'saucy' (rude) and a 'princox' (a cocky youngster). After the ball, Tybalt even follows up his resentment by sending Romeo a letter, challenging him to a fight.

Build critical skills

To what extent does Shakespeare intend his audience to dislike Tybalt, or to view him as a victim of the values of his society?

Shakespeare has Tybalt lurch from one conflict to another, saying that he's 'apt' for fighting Mercutio who calls him a 'rat-catcher' and, mockingly, 'Good King of Cats' in Act 3 scene 1. Mercutio declares that Tybalt is affected, meaning that he keeps up with the modern styles, and implies that he is a 'fashion-monger' (2.4 29). Tybalt taunts Mercutio in Act 3 scene 1 implying, in his use of the word 'consort', that Mercutio follows Romeo around like a wife. The value of honour in Elizabethan England and Verona at the end of the sixteenth century means that it is expected that Tybalt will fight Mercutio when challenged, and when Mercutio is killed Romeo has to gain revenge. There is no great build up to Tybalt's death: he is killed and the story quickly moves on. He has no dying words, which, dramatically speaking, makes the moment of his death less significant than Mercutio's.

Shakespeare gives Tybalt an important role in the play because his violent actions result in the death of one of Romeo's best friends and subsequently cause Romeo's banishment.

Capulet

Shakespeare presents Capulet, head of one of the two rival families in the play, as an authoritative and powerful man. The first time we see him, he is desperate to fight in the brawl at the beginning of Act 1.

He acts as a proud host at his party, chastising Tybalt for wanting to upset events. His desire for authority is emphasised by his comment, 'Am I the master here, or you?' (1.5 77).

Shakespeare highlights Capulet's dramatic change of attitude towards Juliet's marriage. His initial comments in Act 1 scene 2 – such as 'let two more summers whither in their pride/ere we may think her ripe to be a bride' (lines 10–11), that mothers so early made 'are too soon marr'd' (line 13), and 'My will to her consent is but a part...' (line 17) – all attest to his wish to give Juliet time to allow her to make her own choice but he has a marked change of attitude after the murder of Tybalt.

Shakespeare does offer some explanation for Capulet's sudden change of plans for Juliet, by having Lady Capulet explain to Juliet that the 'sudden day of joy' is to lift her from the 'heaviness' of Tybalt's death.

Shakespeare shows Capulet's aggressive and cruel nature when he threatens to throw Juliet out of his house if she refuses to marry Paris. He is furious and says she can 'hang, beg, starve, die in the streets' (3.5 192) if she goes against his wishes. He is so violently angry that even Lady Capulet tells him to calm down. In the context of the play and Elizabethan England, however, the father, as head of a household, did not expect his decisions to be challenged, which explains his reaction to Juliet's disobedience.

The idea that Capulet has brought forward the wedding plans to cheer up Juliet is confirmed by Paris' words to the Friar. He explains that Capulet:

And in his wisdom hastes our marriage

To stop the inundation of her tears.

(4.1 11–12)

However, we must also remember that his family have just been blamed for the death of a kinsman of the Prince (Mercutio), so marrying his daughter to 'a man of wax', highly reputed throughout Verona, would boost his family's honour.

Shakespeare presents Capulet as assuaged by Juliet's later apology for her disobedience and declares, 'My heart is wondrous light' (4.2 45), suggesting that he would prefer her to be happy in her match than force her. Later, he is truly distraught at her supposed death. At the play's denouement, this anguish is repeated, revealing his love for his daughter.

Notably, Shakespeare has Capulet make the first move of peace toward Montague, but note that after Montague promises a statue of pure gold to commemorate Juliet, Capulet equals this with an expensive one for Romeo; possibly to demonstrate that he is equally wealthy.

Lady Capulet

Lady Capulet, Juliet's mother, appears to be a typical female character of this period. She seems dominated by her husband, with whom she has a distant and formal relationship, and while she appears loyal to him on the

Build critical skills

Consider Lady Capulet's comments in Act 1 scene 3 on her own early marriage and subsequent motherhood, along with her attitude to Juliet being married. Note that, as Lady Capulet was Juliet's mother, 'much upon these years' (1.3 73) she can only be about twenty-six now. How does Lady Capulet reflect the marital conventions of the time?

surface, Shakespeare never shows any signs of affection between them. She also has a fairly distant relationship with her daughter but enjoys the luxuries her wealthy lifestyle gives her. She is determined to see her young daughter married to a man of high status in society.

Shakespeare gives Lady Capulet an emotionally charged speech upon the death of Tybalt. Her demand to the Prince, 'For blood of ours, shed blood of Montague' (3.1 140), and her speech in private to Juliet telling of her plans to murder Romeo, have led many modern producers to suggest an illicit affair between Lady Capulet and Tybalt. (This is shown in various ways in both the Luhrmann and Zeffirelli productions.) Indeed, Shakespeare gives her eleven lines of passionate mourning for Tybalt and only the same number for her own daughter when Juliet apparently dies in Act 4 scene 5.

In Act 3 scene 4, Capulet instructs his wife to go and see Juliet and tell her about Paris' love for her. There is a formality about the way he speaks to her, emphasising her subservience and suggesting that their relationship is not necessarily a close one.

When Juliet refuses to marry Paris and asks for her mother to help her, Lady Capulet refuses. This could be interpreted in a number of ways. Shakespeare may be showing her to be afraid to tell her husband of her daughter's disobedience. She could also be considered resentful of her daughter's strength of character in being able to oppose male dominance in a way that she has not. However we read her character here, her inability to do anything practical to help her daughter is clear: in this society, men have control. Lady Capulet sees Juliet is not free to make her own decisions and feels that she must accept, just as she has, the code of practice developed by the men of Renaissance society.

Shakespeare presents Lady Capulet as genuinely upset when Juliet apparently dies in Act 4 scene 5, calling her the 'one thing to rejoice and solace in' (4.5 47), suggesting that Lady Capulet gets little love from her own husband.

Paris

Paris is a good-looking, wealthy young man who wants to marry Juliet. Shakespeare shows that Paris sees nothing unusual about wishing to marry a girl who is not yet 14 and points out that many 'younger than she are happy mothers made'. By having Capulet's approval, he doesn't need Juliet's.

Paris calls Juliet 'his lady' and 'wife' before he has married her. This is a reflection of the degree to which women were meant to fall in line with the wishes of men. Clearly, Paris does not expect any resistance from Juliet. Shakespeare highlights Paris' confidence in the marriage in

Key quotation

Wife, go you to her ere you go to bed;
Acquaint her here of my son Paris' love…
(3.4 15–16)

the fact that he virtually ignores Juliet's unenthusiastic responses to his comments in Act 4 scene 1.

However, Shakespeare shows Paris to be devastated when he thinks that Juliet is dead. He appears, by the standards of the time, to be both honourable and brave in his willingness to protect her final resting place from the insult he imagines Romeo has come to commit. Romeo's words show that even he sees Paris to be a victim of circumstances, and not personally to blame for the tragedy. In allowing Paris some dying words, unlike Tybalt, Shakespeare shows Paris in a positive light, and Romeo agrees to lay Paris beside the woman they both loved, showing the degree to which he respects Paris when he could well have despised him, regarding him as the man who had caused Juliet's death.

Prince Escalus

Prince Escalus (from the word 'scales', which is a symbol associated with justice) is the absolute ruler of Verona as an independent city state. He decides the laws and acts as judge and jury when deciding how justice is to be carried out. This form of justice would have been common at the time of the play. He appears three times in the play. He arrives in Act 1 scene 1 to take control and calm the fight between the feuding families.

Shakespeare also uses him in this scene as a device to tell the audience what has been happening. His language is formal and pompous. He exerts his authority by threatening death if the families brawl again.

In Act 3 scene 1 he banishes Romeo rather than sentencing him to death – he agrees that Romeo's actions were wrong but can also understand the reasons for those actions. He also reveals that Mercutio is related to him and thus his own blood 'lies a-bleeding' as a result of this brawl. This shows a merciful side to his character.

Shakespeare gives the Prince, the character of highest rank, the last words of the play. This both follows the literary convention of the time, and also uses the Prince as a device to underline a moral message. The Prince states that heaven has found ways of punishing them all, including himself who, for 'winking at' (turning a blind eye to) the families' 'discords', has suffered the loss of relations (5.3 294). Shakespeare is showing the audience that the Prince lacks insight into his subjects. Although fate was a contributing factor, the Prince ultimately failed to bring peace to Verona himself.

Montague and Lady Montague

We see the Montagues, the rival family to the Capulets, few times in the play. Lady Montague tries to prevent her husband from joining the fight in Act 1 scene 1 and declares how she is glad her son Romeo was not

Build critical skills

Explain what the Nurse might mean in calling Paris 'a man of wax' (1.3 77). What possible interpretations might this have?

Key quotation

…O give me thy hand, One writ with me in sour misfortune's book! I'll bury thee in a triumphant grave. (5.3 81–83)

Key quotation

Three civil brawls, bred of an airy word By thee, old Capulet, and Montague, Have thrice disturbed the quiet of our streets… (1.1 80–82)

Build critical skills

The Prince has let off the families twice before. What does this suggest about his methods of rule?

Key quotation

O where is Romeo? Saw you him today?
Right glad I am he was not at this fray.
(1.1 108–109)

Key quotation

Alas, my liege, my wife is dead tonight;
Grief of my son's exile hath stopp'd her breath.
(5.3 210–211)

GRADE *FOCUS*

Grade 5

Students will develop a clear understanding of how Shakespeare uses language, form and structure to create characters, supported by appropriate references to the text. Students should show an understanding of the importance of characters, including their link to themes in the play.

Grade 8

Students will examine and evaluate the ways that Shakespeare uses language, form and structure to create characters, supported by carefully chosen and well-integrated references to the text. Students should show a sensitive understanding of the importance of characters, including their link to themes in the play.

at the fight, showing the protective nature of her love for him. She also asks Benvolio to try to find out what is ailing Romeo, again showing her concern for him.

Shakespeare highlights the depth of her love for her son when Montague arrives in the final scene and reveals that his wife has died of a broken heart after Romeo was banished.

That Romeo confides in the Priest rather than his father is not really any surprise. Romeo's disgust at the feud caused by the male heads of the two families is clear when he asks Benvolio what the 'fray' at the start of the play was about, but then quickly adds, 'Yet tell me not ... for I have heard it all.' Shakespeare also has Romeo fail to confide in his mother, possibly because this was not socially acceptable at the time. However, Romeo is clearly a lover of women and this at least hints at a loving relationship with his mother. Remember, Juliet is not the only woman who loves Romeo unto death in the play.

REVIEW YOUR LEARNING

1 Give three adjectives to describe Romeo.
2 Give three adjectives to describe Juliet.
3 Which character says he hates peace?
4 Who is unhappy about Romeo's presence at the Capulet party?
5 Who first mentions marriage in the balcony scene?
6 Which two characters most help to facilitate the lover's secret relationship?
7 Who obstructs Mercutio and Tybalt's fight and inadvertently makes things worse?
8 What is the usual punishment for murder in Veronese society?
9 Who tells Juliet about Tybalt's death and Romeo's banishment?
10 Who supplies Romeo with the poison he uses to kill himself?
Answers on pp. 107–108.

Target your thinking

- What is a theme? (**AO1** and **AO3**)
- What are the main themes in *Romeo and Juliet*? (**AO1** and **AO3**)
- How does Shakespeare present themes in *Romeo and Juliet*? (**AO1** and **AO2**)

In literature, a theme is an idea that a writer explores through the plot, structure, characters and descriptions in the text. It is usually something that the writer wants the audience to think about. Although Shakespeare was writing about issues that were pertinent hundreds of years ago, his themes have universality, which means that their ideas are still relevant to us today.

The key themes in *Romeo and Juliet* are:

- love and relationships
- fate and free will
- youth and age
- friendship and enemies
- families and conflict

Note that there is an overlap between these themes. An essay on youth and age could also bring in families, as the parents in the play seem out of touch with their children. A response on friendship could also consider enemies and thereby address the theme of conflict. However, you should always ensure that your main focus is on the theme that is given in the question.

Love and relationships

Arguably the most important theme of the play is that of love and relationships. The play is full of images of love.

Shakespeare presents different types of love in the play. There is the stylised, courtly love of Romeo's attraction to Rosaline, where Romeo pines away for a woman who ignores his affections. His love is presented as rather affected. Romeo believes himself to be in love and acts as he thinks a rejected lover should – wandering around hopelessly and locking himself in his room. Sexual attraction is also presented here as Romeo is unhappy that Rosaline wants to remain chaste (virginal). He feels that she is wasting her beauty.

In Act 1 scene 4, Romeo debates whether love is tender or rough. In his view, it presents a **dichotomy** and he sums up love's opposing qualities:

> **Key quotation**
>
> *Love is a smoke raised with the fume of sighs, Being purged, a fire sparkling in lovers' eyes...*
> (1.1 181–182)

> **Key quotation**
>
> *Is love a tender thing? it is too rough, Too rude, too boist'rous, and it pricks like thorn.*
> (1.4 25–26)

dichotomy: a contrast between two opposing values or groups.

it can be something gentle and 'tender', but it can also be dangerous. The complexities of love are thereby presented from the play's outset.

Conversely, Mercutio's attitude towards love is entirely negative. He sees it as unmanning Romeo and turning him into an 'ape' or a fool. Mercutio's view of women is entirely sexual and he makes a number of debasing comments in Act 1 scene 4 and Act 2 scenes 1 and 4. Note that Romeo joins in with the sexual puns in scene 4, reflecting the friendship between the two men.

Although there is evidence in the play that Paris loves Juliet, particularly in his reaction to her death in Act 5 scene 3, Juliet clearly does not reciprocate his love. She states, 'He shall not make me there a joyful bride' (3.5 117). Her attitude to marriage, however, is out of line with what is expected from her and this is best exemplified by her father's threats to throw her out of the family home if she refuses to marry Paris. By having Capulet react in such an extreme manner, Shakespeare may be suggesting that this form of arranged marriage is wrong.

The love between Romeo and Juliet is a romantic form of love. Their feelings are deep and there is almost a spirituality about them, conveyed through the religious imagery in their first sonnet in Act 1 scene 5. Their love is passionate but the Friar worries that a hasty relationship leads to 'violent ends'.

The constant advice against passionate and intense love which both Romeo and Juliet are given from family, friends and advisors might be considered the key to the tragic ending of the play. However, it is not just the young, but also the older characters who encourage this union, as both the Nurse and the Friar help the marriage on.

Key quotation

O brawling love,
O loving hate!
(1.1 167)

Key quotation

Therefore love
moderately, long love
doth so;
Too swift arrives as
tardy as too slow.
(2.6 14-15)

GRADE BOOSTER

Thoughtful, successful answers will explore the varied presentations of love in the play. For example, Capulet sees marriage as a commodity and does not object if the couple are not in love. These views are perhaps reflected in his own marriage to Lady Capulet, which is a dutiful rather than loving relationship. This illustrates the business-like attitude to love and marriage which was common in English society in 1595.

Fate and free will

Shakespeare creates and explores his characters' attitudes to the power of fate and destiny, inviting the audience to consider whether they might be rather too quick to reject personal responsibility.

The Prologue pronounces Romeo and Juliet as 'a pair of star-cross'd lovers', but it is significant that the sonnet opens with the human influence – 'Two households' – and the idea of being 'star-crossed' comes later.

It could be argued that Romeo and Juliet's first meeting was destiny. However, Shakespeare stresses Juliet's extreme youth and inexperience, suggesting that she does not know a great deal about love. Furthermore, she has just told her mother that she has not thought about marrying but will do as her mother wishes and 'look to like' Paris (1.3 98). It is notable here, though, that she makes no promises to her mother and is quite clever in her answer, adding that all important 'if looking liking move' (1.3 98). Despite acknowledging the importance of parental consent, that 'gives strength' to 'make [love] fly' (1.3 100), Juliet moves forward in her relationship with Romeo without her parents' knowledge. Juliet says that she 'must love a loathed enemy' (1.5 140) as if she has no choice. However, in Act 2 scene 2, the balcony scene, Juliet tells Romeo that if his intentions are not 'honourable' and his 'purpose marriage', she would rather he left her to her 'grief'. This shows that she is quite capable of choosing whether to take love further or not.

It might also be considered an unfortunate coincidence that the two young lovers happen to be members of the two feuding families, which will cause them great difficulty. But here again, the question is begged as to whose fault it is that the two families are feuding. Not Romeo's or Juliet's, for sure, but not fate, destiny or the stars either. The feud is caused by human forces. The older generation are not good role models in terms of accepting responsibility for their own actions: old Montague and Capulet with their petty feud, the Friar with his meddling and the Nurse with her childishly enthusiastic involvement in orchestrating Juliet's 'love' life.

It could be argued that 'fate' ensures that the Friar's letter to Romeo is not delivered, but had it not been for the Friar's plan in the first place, there would have been no need for the letter. The Friar marries the lovers without their parents' permission, in the knowledge that this would not be accepted by either family, yet he does not blame himself for the final tragedy and talks instead of 'an unkind hour', 'chance', 'accident' and 'untimely' events in Act 5 scene 3.

Romeo certainly blames fate for events, sensing a 'consequence yet hanging in the stars' (1.5 107) before attending the Capulet ball, lamenting that he is 'fortune's fool' (3.1 127) after killing Tybalt and ranting 'then I defy you, stars!' after learning of Juliet's death in Act 5 scene 1. Arguably, fate's biggest role is when Romeo kills himself just before Juliet wakes up. Even here, though, one can't help but wonder whether Shakespeare did not intend us to see that, had the impetuous Romeo sought out the Friar first to hear what had happened, the ending would have been different.

This is a tragedy and so Shakespeare will have intended us to see the outcome as anything but the result of a single cause, be it an outside force such as destiny, or an internal one such as a personal characteristic. Rather, the tragedy evolves through the complex intertwining of many different factors.

It is interesting that, at the end of the play, the Prince and old Montague and Capulet do finally accept their responsibility for having set the tragedy in motion. The Prince recognises his error in 'winking at' (turning a blind eye to) their 'discords' (5.3 294) and Capulet and Montague acknowledge blame for the feud that has caused them to lose their children. The play ends with the idea that social harmony is restored only when personal responsibility is accepted.

GRADE BOOSTER

When writing about fate, candidates should consider Shakespeare's decision to actually reveal the play's ending in the Prologue. The audience thereby knows from the outset that Romeo and Juliet will die at the end of the play. Every time a character feels threatened by fate, the audience gets to feel more knowledgeable than them.

Youth and age

The different viewpoints and behaviour of older and younger characters results in many of the tensions of the play. It was the older generation's 'ancient grudge' which set the feud in motion (Prologue 3). Even as an older man, Capulet still wishes to involve himself in the first brawl and calls for his sword, leading to his wife's mockery that a crutch might be more appropriate given his advancing years. He later acknowledges that men 'so old' as he and Montague should be able to 'keep the peace' (Act 1 scene 2).

The relationships between children and their parents are part of the theme of youth and age. Romeo's parents are unaware of the reason for their son's recent sadness and Montague says that he can 'neither know it, nor can learn of him' (1.1 135) as Romeo is reluctant to share his feelings. Instead, he shares them with Benvolio. Similarly, the Capulets remain ignorant of Juliet's real feelings towards Paris until Act 3 scene 5. Capulet initially considers whether Juliet is too young to marry and would be 'marred' (1.2 13) by early motherhood but when she later refuses in Act 3 scene 5, her pleas for leniency are ignored and she is threatened with violence and rejection, showing that power in the play lies with the older generation. We recall that Juliet 'hath not seen the change of fourteen years' (1.2 9) and would be expected to obey her parents without question. In this, she is much closer to the Nurse than her parents, and this could be partly due to the Nurse's childish enthusiasm which is closer to Juliet's own outlook. Yet the difference between youth and age is still marked here, particularly in Act 2 scene 5 when the Nurse's slow return with Romeo's message agitates Juliet and leads to disparaging comments about age.

The lovers turn to the older Friar for advice and guidance. His warnings not to hasten into a relationship are ignored, although he doesn't practise what he preaches and marries them swiftly after Romeo's request.

The Prologue to Act 2 reminds us that it is the love of two young people that is at the heart of the play.

Juliet's desire for Romeo before their wedding night reminds us of her youth. Romeo is not much older than Juliet and this is highlighted in his childish reaction to his banishment. He refuses to listen to the Friar's calming words and, instead, falls on the floor crying.

In the play's closing scene, Montague feels that 'woe conspires' against his age and stresses how unnatural it is for a child to die before their parent. Looking on his son, he laments, 'what manners is in this/To press before thy father to a grave?' (5.3 214–215).

> **Key quotation**
>
> *But old folks, many feign as they were dead, Unwieldy, slow, heavy, and pale as lead.*
> (2.5 16–17)

> **Key quotation**
>
> *Now old desire doth in his death-bed lie, And young affection gapes to be his heir.*
> (2.P 1–2)

GRADE BOOSTER

```
Remember that themes can overlap, so an essay on youth
and age might also touch upon the theme of conflict.
This doesn't mean that you can ignore your question's
given theme and write about another theme that you
have spent more time revising - your examiner will
soon notice this - but by considering linked themes,
you can add depth to your essay's argument.
```

Friendship and enemies

There are strong loyalties in *Romeo and Juliet*. Romeo, Mercutio and Benvolio are good friends, despite their differences. Benvolio seeks peace, Mercutio is argumentative and Romeo is lovesick. Romeo deserts the group, first for Rosaline, then for Juliet, but comes back to his friends at points in the play and avenges Mercutio's death against Tybalt.

Romeo confides his feelings about Rosaline to Benvolio, and this is clearly something Benvolio expects, saying that he is otherwise 'much denied' (1.1 148). On a few occasions Mercutio is seen to be concerned as to where Romeo is, including at the beginning of Act 2 scene 4, when he declares, 'Where the dev'l should this Romeo be?' Some literary critics have suggested that Mercutio is in love with Romeo and put forward the idea that Mercutio uses his Queen Mab fairy story to

Build critical skills

Think about how Shakespeare uses characters to present particular themes. For example, how does he present the theme of friendship through Mercutio? Can you think of other characters that are used in this way?

Build critical skills

To what extent could the relationships between the Friar and Romeo, and Juliet and the Nurse be considered friendships?

Key quotation

O brother Montague, give me thy hand… (5.3 296)

seduce Romeo but Romeo does not understand and Mercutio gives up, frustrated, admitting that he talks 'of dreams' (1.4 96). Note that this is just one possible interpretation.

While Romeo's friendships are strong, the rivalry with the Capulets has damaging strength. This rivalry permeates all areas of Veronese society. The play even opens with an argument between the servants of the two families. Throughout the play, there is a threat of violence from Tybalt's continual attempts to cause chaos, whether it is at Capulet's party in Act 1 scene 5 or on the streets in Act 1 scene 1 and Act 3 scene 1.

Romeo does not want any part in the feud and walks away from the violence in Act 3 scene 1. We know this is because of his marriage to Juliet, but he cannot tell anyone else this, which causes Mercutio to step in to defend Romeo's honour. It is ironic that by trying to stop the fight, Romeo unwittingly causes the death of his close friend. Romeo also does not tell his friends about Juliet. They continue to think that he remains in love with Rosaline.

Families and conflict

Shakespeare presents conflict both between families and within families. (See 'Youth and age' on p. 50 for a discussion of conflict between parents and children.) Shakespeare opens both the Prologue and the first scene of the play with a focus on the feud. There is a juxtaposition of opposite emotions as strong love forms against this backdrop of hate.

The power of a family name, and what it represents, obsesses the characters. In Act 1 scene 1, Sampson says 'A dog of the house of Montague moves' him and Tybalt declares that he hates 'all Montagues' and seems convinced that the family are out to destroy the Capulets.

In Act 1 scene 5 Juliet asks herself, 'wherefore [why] art thou Romeo' because she knows that his name will cause problems. The strength of the feud means that only the deaths of the lovers, Montague's wife and Paris can convince Capulet and Montague that it must come to an end.

Family values are different in the world of the play from those we see today. This is most evident in Shakespeare's portrayal of the Capulet family. In Act 3 scene 5, Capulet asks his wife if she has delivered his 'decree' to Juliet regarding whom she will marry. Shakespeare's choice of word clearly underlines that Capulet sees his wishes as law. This repressive existence results in Juliet lying to them and disobeying her parents because she is in love with Romeo.

Shakespeare leaves his audience with some hope at the end of the play that Verona can now be a peaceful place. The feud, arguably, has caused the lovers to marry in secret, Tybalt and Mercutio's deaths, the brawl in Act 1 scene 1 and, we are told by the Prince, at least two other fights before the action of the play commences (1.1 80). The feud seems ever-present, either in the background or as the centre of the action, causing Romeo's banishment and the Friar's plans, and ultimately resulting in the deaths of Romeo and Juliet.

GRADE BOOSTER

Successful answers might explore how Romeo is presented as part of a friendship group, rather than with his immediate family. This distances him from the feud and family issues in the play as he seems independent of his parents. By contrast, Juliet is in her family home for most of the play.

GRADE FOCUS

Grade 5

Students will be able to show a clear understanding of the key themes of the play and how Shakespeare uses language, form and structure to explore them, supported by appropriate references to the text.

Grade 8

Students will be able to examine and evaluate the key themes of the play, analysing the ways that Shakespeare uses language, form and structure to explore them. Comments will be supported by carefully chosen and well-integrated references to the text.

REVIEW YOUR LEARNING

1 What is a theme?
2 What are the main themes in *Romeo and Juliet*?
3 What characters are used to explore the theme of love and relationships?
4 What other theme(s) might an essay on youth and age link to?
5 Who does Romeo confide in rather than his parents?
6 What other theme(s) might an essay on friendship and enemies link to?
7 In what way is the final tragedy partly the Prince's fault?
8 Consider whether each of the main themes are relevant in society today.

Answers on p. 108.

Target your thinking

- How does Shakespeare use stagecraft to reveal the story and themes of *Romeo and Juliet*? (**AO2**)
- What use does Shakespeare make of poetry and prose? (**AO2**)
- How does Shakespeare use imagery and symbolism in *Romeo and Juliet*? (**AO2**)
- How does Shakespeare create atmospheric settings in the play? (**AO2**)

You will notice from the questions above that when analysing language and style the Assessment Objective with which we are most concerned is AO2. This refers to the writer's methods and is usually highlighted in the exam question by the word 'how'.

Examiners report that AO2 is often the most overlooked by students in the examination. For example, candidates who fail to address AO2 often write about the characters in a text as if they are real people involved in real events rather than analysing them as 'constructs' or creations of the writer.

To succeed at AO2, you must deal effectively with the writer's use of language, form and structure. Turn to p. 34 for analysis of the structure of *Romeo and Juliet*.

GRADE *BOOSTER*

It is not enough to simply identify the methods used by a writer. You must analyse the effects on the audience produced by these features.

Tragedy and comedy

Romeo and Juliet is different from Shakespeare's other tragedies in that it becomes a tragedy rather than starts as one. Despite the ominous tone of the Prologue and the early street fight, there are comic moments. Capulet calls for his sword as his wife taunts, 'A crutch, a crutch! Why call you for a sword?' (1.1 67) Mercutio's wit is lively and engaging and he and Romeo joke together in Act 2 scene 4. The humour gives the audience an insight into what Veronese society could be, were it not for the feud. This highlights the play's tragedy rather than detracts from it. The **juxtaposition** of humour and tragedy also conveys the chaos of this society.

juxtaposition: two contrasting things placed side by side.

This sort of juxtapositioning of comic and serious scenes is common to tragedies of this period. Shakespeare is using stagecraft to offer 'relief' to the audience from the serious and tragic elements of the play. It is important to note, though, that the comic scenes do normally reflect the serious themes of the play. For example, the sexual innuendos of Sampson and Gregory at the start of the play are at odds with the serious treatment of love that we see between Romeo and Juliet. In another contrast, Benvolio and Mercutio mock Romeo's passionate nature throughout Act 1 and Act 2 scenes 1 and 4, whereas Juliet takes it seriously.

In the same way, the thumb-biting incident of Act 1 scene 1 is a reflection of just how petty the original cause of the feud is, highlighted shortly afterwards when the Prince tells us it has been caused by, or 'bred of', a careless 'airy word' (1.1 80). Shakespeare uses the lower characters to parody the behaviour of the higher characters in the play. This, again, was a common literary device of the time and one which an Elizabethan audience would have been familiar with.

Shakespeare uses wit to enhance tragic events. The tragi-comedy of Mercutio's dying lines, 'Ask for me tomorrow, and you shall find me a grave man' (3.1 89) makes his death more poignant as he attempts a joke before he dies. The play becomes more serious after this point. However, Shakespeare was aware that he was writing to entertain his audience and not to depress, so the supposed death of Juliet in Act 4 scene 5 and the mourning of her family is followed with a brief, lively argument between Peter and the musicians. The lively tone seems out of place and, indeed, some directors choose to cut the scene, but the quick dialogue offers light relief from the intense focus on Romeo and Juliet's relationship.

> **GRADE** *BOOSTER*
>
> Don't neglect the comic scenes in the play. You will boost your grade if you can explore how Shakespeare uses them to enhance tragic events, convey the idea of chaos and reflect the more serious themes of the play.

The Chorus

The Chorus operates in a similar way to a third-person narrative voice in a novel, where an omniscient (all-powerful, all-seeing) voice can see precisely what is motivating the characters that are under discussion.

The Prologue

The Prologue, spoken by the Chorus at the start of the play, is a kind of foreword and is written in **sonnet form**. Each of the three **quatrains** (set of four lines) provides a succinct opportunity to sum up an important aspect of the story:

- First quatrain: two families of equally high ranking in Verona have had a quarrel for many years. Now it will erupt afresh and much blood will be shed.
- Second quatrain: a child is born to each family, the children fall in love and their deaths end the quarrel.
- Third quatrain: how all of this unfolds – their love, their parents' anger and finally the end of the quarrel, will be shown during the ensuing two hours of the play.

The final two lines, a **rhyming couplet**, neatly emphasise an important point: the noise levels common in the Elizabethan theatre would have made it difficult for many in the audience to hear the dialogue of the play, hence the suggestion that if they 'with patient ears attend/What *here* shall miss, [the actors'] toil shall strive to mend'. The **pun** on the word 'here' suggests that if they cannot *hear* the storyline from the Prologue, they should be able to understand what is going on from watching the action of the play carefully.

We also see the Chorus providing commentary on the characters at the start of Act 2.

Shakespeare uses the Chorus to emphasise that Romeo's 'love' for women is driven by the way in which they look. Not only this, but the words 'That fair for which loved groaned for and would die' refer not to Romeo's willingness to die for Juliet, but for Rosaline at the play's outset.

Romeo's immediate attraction to Juliet in Act 1 has already shown that he falls in love quickly, but the Chorus' statements are still significant. Through the Chorus, Shakespeare tells us that Romeo and Juliet's 'passion lends them power' and they will need to overcome the obstacles in their way.

Verse and prose

Shakespeare followed certain theatrical conventions when writing his plays. The characters speak in either poetry (verse) or prose (normal speech). Characters lower in rank speak mostly in prose, for example, servants such as Sampson and Gregory in Act 1 scene 1, the serving men in Act 1 scene 5 and the musicians in Act 4 scene 5. Characters higher in rank, such as the Prince, Capulet, Romeo and Juliet, speak in verse. This makes these characters sound more important and intelligent. It should be noted, however, that in certain scenes, Mercutio most notably speaks not in verse but in prose which stresses his disturbed state of mind when he is fretting about Romeo, such as in Act 2 scene 4. Prose is also used in

Key quotation

That fair for which love groaned for and would die,
With tender Juliet matched is now not fair.
Now Romeo is beloved, and loves again,
Alike bewitchèd by the charm of looks…
(2.P 3–6)

Build critical skills

Look at the verbs Shakespeare uses in the Prologue to Act 2 to describe the way Romeo falls in love. What do they tell you about his attitude to love?

Mercutio's fight with Tybalt in Act 3 scene 1 and when he is injured in this scene, conveying his agitation.

The lines of verse contain about **ten syllables**. In his verse, Shakespeare uses **iambic pentameter** which consists of five unstressed beats and five stressed beats. For instance:

– ./   –   /   –   /   – /   –   /

But, soft! what light through yonder window breaks?

Actors do not emphasise these beats when they speak as this would sound unnatural, but this was the conventional writing style of this period.

Imagery

Imagery is visually descriptive language that literally creates an 'image' for the audience. Through this, Shakespeare uses description, allusion, similes and metaphors to appeal to the senses. Imagery can be used to bring events alive, illuminate characters or enhance our understanding of themes. Shakespeare also uses symbols to convey ideas. Characters, events and even objects represent wider ideas in the play. Some of the play's images are particularly striking and their ideas are drawn out over several lines. This is called a conceit. One example is in Act 1 scene 3 lines 82–93, when Lady Capulet compares Paris to a book that Juliet would delight in reading. Here, the book image is continued for twelve lines.

> **GRADE** *BOOSTER*
>
> ```
> An analysis of Shakespeare's use of imagery is vital if
> your exam board asks you to look closely at an extract.
> Exploring imagery will gain you valuable marks in AO2
> because you will be looking at the craft of the writer.
> ```

Light and dark imagery

Images of dark and light bring the play to life and lend an aesthetic quality to the staging. Players at the Globe had few props or scenery as these were very expensive and difficult to make. Instead, sights and sounds were described. Lightning, torches, the 'inconstant' moon and rising sun are all referenced in the play. One of Romeo's first lines on seeing Juliet is, 'O she doth teach the torches to burn bright!' (1.5 43.) The idea of Juliet as a source of light is further conveyed in the balcony scene. Shakespeare has Romeo use the metaphor of Juliet as a 'bright angel', whilst creeping round under 'night's cloak' in the dark of the Capulet gardens.

Build critical skills

Why does Shakespeare use prose at certain points in *Romeo and Juliet*?

Key quotation

But soft, what light through yonder window breaks?
It is the east, and Juliet is the sun.
(2.2 2–3)

Build critical skills

How does Shakespeare have Romeo use imagery of light to describe his first sight of Juliet in Act 1 scene 5?

Build critical skills

How does imagery of darkness and light help us to understand Romeo's character in the balcony scene? Consider how he is willing to risk death just to see Juliet.

Key quotation

...bring in cloudy night immediately.
Spread thy close curtain, love-performing Night.
(3.2 4–5)

Key quotation

A glooming peace this morning with it brings,
The sun for sorrow will not show his head.
(5.3 305–306)

▲ Juliet on the balcony in the Luhrmann adaptation

On her wedding night, Juliet personifies nightfall to hasten the darkness that will bring Romeo to her room.

Just as Romeo considers Juliet to be a source of light, so Juliet considers Romeo as a light that illuminates the darkness. He can be 'cut ... out in little stars' so that 'all the world will be in love with night' (3.2 24). On the following morning, light works against the lovers as Romeo must leave for Mantua at daybreak and fears, 'More light and light, more dark and dark our woes!' (3.5 36) At the play's denouement, Juliet's beauty lights the dark tomb for Romeo as 'her beauty makes/This vault a feasting presence full of light.' (5.3 85–86) Although the lovers marry in the day, their happiest moments take place at night as each regards the other as a source of light in their lives. This turns to sorrow in the final night-time scene. The enormity of the lovers' deaths even has an effect on nature as the Prince doubts whether the sun will rise after such tragic events.

Death imagery

The background of the feud means that death is never far away in the play and the Prologue highlights this from the outset. The world of Verona is a dangerous place, where its citizens die young and speak of being 'death-marked' (Prologue 9) and seen by a 'death-darting eye' (3.2 47). Romeo senses 'untimely death' (1.5 111) as he goes to the Capulets' ball, but risks his life in Juliet's garden and considers that a challenge to 'love-devouring Death' is worth it (2.6 7). The lovers' dark future hangs over them continually. They both contemplate suicide after Romeo's banishment and Juliet claims she would leap 'From off the battlements of any tower' (4.1 78) to avoid marrying Paris, thereby confirming to the Friar that she would be willing to feign death to avoid an unwelcome marriage. Juliet fears that Romeo is already dead to her when he leaves her room after their wedding night and she gazes down at him, 'As one dead in the bottom of a tomb' (3.5 55–56) in a stark foreshadowing of the play's denouement.

Despite Capulet's acceptance after Tybalt's death that 'we were born to die' (3.4 4), he is distraught at his own daughter's supposed death. In Act 4 scene 5, Shakespeare personifies Death as a cruel bridegroom that has 'lain with' Juliet (line 36). Her family rail against 'cruel Death' (line 48) and 'detestable Death' (line 56) that is seen as a mighty force.

The final image of death in Act 5 scene 3 is haunting. Romeo looks on the Capulet vault and regards it as consuming Juliet's body.

Key quotation

Thou detestable maw, thou womb of death, Gorged with the dearest morsel of the earth...
(5.3 45–46)

GRADE *BOOSTER*

```
Remember that cross-referencing characters, events and
effects proves that you know the play well and will
help you gain extra marks. In the final scene, Romeo
speaks to the 'dead' Juliet and considers:
   ...the lean abhorred monster keeps
   Thee here in dark to be his paramour...
   (5.3 103-105)
Consider what he means and where else in the play a
similar idea has been used.
```

Build critical skills

Aside from Romeo and Juliet, which other characters in the play are linked with death?

The deaths of Romeo and Juliet send shockwaves through Veronese society but perhaps the play's greatest contradiction is that the ultimate result of so many deaths is peace.

Disease imagery

Disease imagery is used throughout the play and lends a negative undertone to the language. When the Prince berates Capulet and Montague for their 'civil brawls', he describes their hands as 'cankered' (1.1 85–86), meaning diseased.

In Act 1 scene 1 Romeo says he feels diseased and 'sick' because he has been rejected by Rosaline. He feels so 'ill' he needs to make a will in case he dies, yet he still has the wit to point out how the word 'ill' sounds similar to 'will', which makes him feel worse:

Bid a sick man in sadness make his will –

A word ill urged to one that is so ill.

(1.1 193–194)

Benvolio tells Romeo that love is like an eye infection and the only way for the poison of the old infection (his love for Rosaline) to 'die' (be cured) is to get a 'new infection', meaning a new love. Using the word 'infection' implies that, even with a new love, Romeo will still be diseased, showing what Benvolio considers to be the danger of love.

The idea of sickness is also juxtaposed against the beauty of Juliet. In Act 2 scene 2, Romeo compares her to the 'fair sun' (line 4), something that gives light and life, and contrasts her with the 'envious' moon, which looks 'pale' (line 5) and unwell.

Religious imagery

Shakespeare uses imagery to link religion with love throughout the play. When Romeo and Juliet meet for the first time in Act 1 scene 5 they describe the act of kissing as saintly. Romeo begins the imagery of 'pilgrims' and a 'holy shrine', elevating the nature of his love for Juliet to the status of a pure and holy quest. He uses this imagery to steal a kiss from Juliet. She encourages the kiss by joining in with the imagery of 'palmers' (pilgrims who brought a palm leaf back from their visit) but still behaves a little shyly by suggesting that pilgrims use their hands to make contact, not their lips.

Romeo describes their first kiss as like a prayer, saying that kissing Juliet feels as if her pure lips have taken away all his sins:

Then move not, while my prayer's effect I take.

Thus from my lips, by yours, my sin is purged.

(1.5 105–106)

Romeo and Juliet's first dialogue in Act 1 scene 5 lines 92–105 is structured as a sonnet.

- First quatrain: Romeo's first words to Juliet use religious imagery of pilgrims in a proposal to kiss her.
- Second quatrain: Juliet's response is encouraging but also shy as she points out that pilgrims touch hands, not lips.
- Third quatrain: the lovers share lines here to discuss pilgrims' behaviour. Note that the shared lines signal the lovers moving closer, both physically and emotionally.

The final two lines are a rhyming couplet and the lovers speak one each of these paired lines, reflecting their closeness.

Key quotation

Good pilgrim, you do wrong your hand too much, Which mannerly devotion shows in this, For saints have hands that pilgrims' hands do touch, And palm to palm is holy palmers' kiss. (1.5 96–99)

Build critical skills

Remember that cross-referencing characters, events and techniques is a skill that shows your confidence with the text. How is Romeo's language when speaking to Juliet in Act 1 scene 5 different from the language he uses in Act 1 scene 1 when talking about Rosaline?

Symbolism

A symbol is something that the playwright uses to represent an idea.

Bird symbolism

In augury (forecasting the future from signs in nature) birds were seen as extremely important and Shakespeare often uses symbols of birds to illustrate his points. Birds were seen as warnings of fate, which reflects the superstitious nature of society at the time.

Benvolio tries to cheer up Romeo in Act 1 scene 2, telling him: 'I will make thee think thy swan a crow' (line 87). He means that the girls at the Capulets' party will make Rosaline, who Romeo thinks is like a beautiful and graceful swan, seem like an ugly crow. It is significant that the crow was a bird thought to foreshadow death. This is ironic, in that it is Romeo's love for Juliet, the 'swan', that leads to his death and not his love for Rosaline.

Falconry (hunting with birds of prey) was popular in Elizabethan times and Shakespeare uses the idea of the huntsman and bird in Act 2 scene 2. Juliet calls Romeo from her window and wishes for the falconer's voice 'To lure this tassel-gentle back again' (line 158) – to call Romeo as the huntsman lures the bird. Romeo enquires, 'My niesse?' (line 167), calling Juliet by the name used for a young hawk, suggesting her youth. Juliet wishes Romeo were only a small distance away, 'no farther than a wanton's bird' (line 177), meaning a child's pet bird that only 'hop(s) a little from his hand' (line 178). Romeo agrees, 'I would I were thy bird' (line 182) and Juliet extends this image, saying she would look after him so much that she would kill him: 'Yet I should kill thee with much cherishing.' (2.2 183) Shakespeare's use of language in this scene shows the irony of Romeo's love for Juliet leading to both their deaths.

In Act 3 scene 5, the lark, a bird of the dawn, takes on a negative association as it heralds the separation of the lovers. Normally it would be a good sign, as night ending and light returning was usually seen as a positive event.

Crude language and puns

The crude language used in the play would have been seen as a huge source of humour for the audience. Actors would certainly have exaggerated the rude jokes to achieve maximum impact in front of a rowdy audience.

The many sexual **innuendos** and **puns** (words with more than one meaning) create a comic ambiguity, flattering the intelligence of the audience and inviting them to laugh. For example, the double meaning

Key quotation

Some say the lark makes sweet division; This doth not so, for she divideth us.
(3.5 29–30)

Build critical skills

How does Shakespeare's use of symbolism aid our understanding of Elizabethan beliefs and interests?

of Gregory's line, 'draw thy tool...' (1.1 28), and Sampson's response, 'my naked weapon is out', takes little imagination to work out. Some of Mercutio's double entendres are slightly more difficult to interpret, but all of them make sex sound dirty and do not have much to do with Romeo's romantic notions of love.

Build critical skills

When you are analysing Shakespeare's use of imagery, it is important to look closely at his language choices. Consider the significance of Mercutio's words to Benvolio in Act 2 scene 1, which he hopes that the hidden Romeo will hear. Explain the puns and innuendos in Mercutio's speech. What do they suggest about Mercutio's character? (See *Characterisation* p. 38.)

Note that Shakespeare does not just use crude humour for a quick laugh. Rather, the humour reveals something about his themes. The crude and bawdy language of love is contrasted with the highly poetic language of love used by Romeo and Juliet. In spite of the high nature of their language, their love still appears to be founded upon physical attraction. (See *Plot and structure* sections on Mercutio's crude comments in Act 2 scene 1 and Act 2 scene 4 and more romantic love looked at in sections on Act 1 scene 5, Act 2 scene 2, Act 3 scene 2 and Act 3 scene 5. See *Characterisation* sections on Romeo, Juliet and Mercutio, and 'Love and relationships' in *Themes*.)

Oxymorons and antithesis

Shakespeare uses many oxymorons in *Romeo and Juliet*. An **oxymoron** is a phrase that contains contradictory words. The effect is often used to show conflict in feelings. Romeo uses a number of oxymorons in Act 1 scene 1. He is confused about love as he adores Rosaline but she is not interested. The opposites of 'brawling love', 'loving hate' (line 167) and 'heavy lightness' (line 169) convey his bewilderment.

When Juliet says good night to Romeo at the end of Act 2 scene 2, she thinks that their 'parting' is 'sweet' in that they will soon be together again, but she is still sorry as she does not want to be apart from him:

Good night, good night! Parting is such sweet sorrow…

(2.2 184)

Key quotation

Feather of lead, bright smoke, cold fire, sick health.
(1.1 171)

Build critical skills

In Act 3 scene 2, Shakespeare has Juliet use many oxymorons to describe Romeo after he has killed Tybalt. She calls Romeo 'A damnèd saint, an honourable villain!' (3.2 79) and questions

Was ever book containing such vile matter

So fairly bound? O that deceit should dwell

In such a gorgeous palace!

(3.2 83–85)

What opposing ideas are introduced here and how do they reveal Juliet's feelings for Romeo at this point?

antithesis (plural antitheses): a person or thing that is the direct opposite of something else.

Build critical skills

Read Friar Lawrence's first speech in Act 2 scene 3 lines 1–30 and find as many examples of antitheses as you can. What is Shakespeare suggesting?

There are extended **antitheses** after Juliet's death in Act 4 scene 5. After preparing for her wedding, the family now switch to make arrangements for her funeral. Capulet sets the idea of a wedding's happy festival against the darkness of a funeral.

All things we ordained festival,

Turn from their office to black funeral.

(4.5 84–85)

Rhyming couplets

Many of the scenes in *Romeo and Juliet* end with rhyming couplets, a technique Shakespeare often used to signal the end of a phase of action. Note that the original performances of his plays were not divided into the 'five acts containing several scenes' formula that we see today. Juliet's last lines to Romeo in Act 2 scene 2 end with a rhyming couplet, as do Romeo's, to indicate to the audience that is the end of their meeting:

Hence will I to my ghostly sire's close cell,

His help to crave, and my dear hap to tell.

(2.2 188–189)

Rhyming couplets are also used to emphasise important points or moments in the play. Rhyme works as a memory aid and often the words with the most important meanings are those that rhyme at the end of the lines. In this way, Shakespeare ensures that his meaning has impact on the audience. The Prince ends the play with a rhyming couplet to summarise events succinctly:

For never was a story of more woe

Than this of Juliet and her Romeo.

(5.3 309–310)

Build critical skills

How does Shakespeare have Juliet use repetition in her Act 2 scene 2 speech, lines 33–36 and 38–49, and how does it emphasise Juliet's feelings of confusion here?

Repetition

There are many examples of repetition in the play, a tactic used to emphasise certain feelings and ideas. Juliet repeats Romeo's name several times in Act 2 scene 2:

> O Romeo, Romeo, wherefore art thou Romeo?
>
> (2.2 33)

The constant repetition of 'name' in her following speech (lines 38–49) shows how aggrieved she feels that Romeo is a Montague, and therefore a great enemy of her family.

In Act 4 scene 5 the repetition of 'look', 'O me!' and 'help!' shows the desperation in both Lady Capulet and the Nurse's reactions to Juliet's death, showing how much she means to her family.

Pace

Time and pace are referred to on a number of occasions in the play. When in love with Rosaline, Romeo mourns that 'sad hours seem long' (1.1 152). By contrast, his initial meeting with Juliet is brief before 'it waxes late' (1.5 125) and the Capulet ball ends. Time seems to stand still in the Capulet orchard as the lovers exchange their vows. Juliet feels that their love is 'too rash, too unadvised, too sudden' (2.2 118–120) yet still laments 'tis twenty years' (2.2 169) until the anticipated message from Romeo the next morning. The Friar warns that Romeo should move 'Wisely and slow' in affairs of love because 'they stumble that run fast' (2.3 94). When the Nurse's return with the morning's message takes her three hours, Juliet becomes frustrated because she feels that love should move quickly.

Morning comes too quickly for the couple after their secret wedding night. Juliet tries to persuade herself 'It was the nightingale, and not the lark' (3.5 2) that wakes them. The pressure of time means Romeo must make a hasty exit – Juliet's mother is calling and he has only a few hours to get to Mantua. The speed of events then forces the lovers' hasty actions. Capulet's decision to bring the wedding forward means Juliet 'wonder(s) at this haste' (3.5 118) and needs to take the sleeping drug sooner that she originally intended. News of her supposed death sends Romeo rushing back to Verona. The fact that Romeo kills himself just before Juliet awakes seems especially cruel timing, with the Friar bemoaning the 'unkind hour' (5.3 145) that caused this. Shakespeare's clever use of pace adds dramatic immediacy to events in the play.

Irony

Irony is used throughout the play. **Dramatic irony** is created whenever the audience is aware of something that the players on the stage are

Key quotation

Therefore do nimble-pinioned doves draw Love,
And therefore hath the wind-swift Cupid wings.
(2.5 7–8)

not. For example, it is ironic that Juliet responds to Paris greeting her as his 'wife' with the words 'that may be sir, when I may be a wife' (4.1 19). Paris thinks she means that he may call her wife when they are actually married, but we know her to mean that she can't be his wife as she is already married. Irony is particularly marked when Juliet's family are mourning over her apparently dead body in Act 4 scene 5. Juliet's apparent death also heightens the poignancy of Romeo's needless suicide. Before he takes the poison, he even remarks on how alive she looks, with the 'crimson in [her] lips and ... cheeks' (5.3 95).

The effect of dramatic irony is to heighten the emotion of the final tragedy as we deduce that characters' happy moments will not last long. It also puts the audience a step ahead of the characters in understanding events better than they do. The audience enjoys this position of privilege.

Build critical skills

Read Romeo's speech in Act 5 scene 3 lines 91–105 and find as many examples of irony as you can.

Settings

Remember that players at the Globe had few props and scenery. Consequently, Shakespeare may state where a setting is, but he barely describes it as the actors would not have been able to build the corresponding set. Instead, description of scenes encourages the audience to use their imagination to visualise where the action is set. The play opens with a reference to setting as the audience are told that they are looking at 'fair Verona'. Romeo sneaks into the Capulet garden in Act 2 scene 2 and we are told by Juliet that 'The orchard walls are high and hard to climb' (line 63) and that it is night because Romeo has 'night's cloak' (line 75) to hide him. He cannot see Juliet blush because 'the mask of night' hides her face (line 85). A clear evocation of setting is presented in Act 4 scene 3 when Juliet imagines waking in the Capulet tomb and seeing 'the bones' of her 'buried ancestors' (lines 40 and 41). Shakespeare employs the senses for Juliet to describe the sight of Tybalt's corpse, 'fest'ring in his shroud' (line 43), the 'loathsome smells' (line 46), the sound of 'shrieks like mandrakes' torn out of the earth' (line 47) and touch of 'forefather's joints' (line 51) that will send her mad. Although she is not actually in the tomb yet, it prepares both Juliet and the audience for the final scene there.

GRADE *BOOSTER*

Merely mentioning that Shakespeare uses any of these devices of language and style will not gain you a good mark. You need to show the examiner that you understand *how* the device works. In other words, how does it achieve Shakespeare's desired effect on the audience?

GRADE *FOCUS*

Grade 5

Students will be able to show a clear appreciation of the techniques Shakespeare uses to create effects for the audience, supported by appropriate references to the text.

Grade 8

Students will be able to explore and analyse the techniques that Shakespeare uses to create effects for the audience, supported by carefully chosen and well-integrated references to the text.

REVIEW YOUR LEARNING

1 How could *Romeo and Juliet* be described as a tragi-comedy?

2 How does Shakespeare use the Chorus in the play?

3 What is imagery?

4 What poetic form does Shakespeare use for the lovers' first dialogue?

5 Which character uses disease imagery to describe love as an 'infection'?

6 The Prince uses imagery of darkness in the play's closing lines. What does he say?

7 Which type of characters in the play speak in poetry and which in prose, and why?

8 Why does Shakespeare have Romeo use oxymorons when he speaks of his feelings for Rosaline?

9 How does Shakespeare's use of light imagery in Act 5 scene 3 convey Romeo's thoughts on Juliet's beauty?

10 Why does Shakespeare sometimes use crude language in *Romeo and Juliet*?

Answers on p. 108.

Target your thinking

- What sorts of questions will you have to answer?
- What is the best way to plan and structure your answer?
- How can you improve your grade?
- What do you have to do to achieve the highest grade?

Your response to a question on *Romeo and Juliet* will be assessed in a 'closed book' English Literature examination, which means that you are not allowed to take copies of the text into the examination room. Different examination boards will test you in different ways and it is vital that you know what the expectations are for your examination board so that you can be well-prepared on the day of the exam.

Whichever board you are following, the table on the next page explains which paper and section the question appears in and gives you information about the sort of question you will face and how you will be assessed.

Marking

The marking of your responses varies according to the board your school or you have chosen. Each exam board will have a slightly different mark scheme, consisting of a ladder of grades. The marks you achieve in each part of the examination will be converted to your final overall grade. Grades are numbered from 1–9, with 9 being the highest.

It is important that you familiarise yourself with the relevant mark scheme(s) for your examination. After all, how can you do well unless you know exactly what is required?

Assessment Objectives for individual assessment are explained in the next section of the guide (see p. 77).

Approaching the examination question

First impressions

First read the whole question and make sure you understand *exactly* what the task requires you to do. It is very easy in the highly pressured atmosphere of the examination room to misread a question and this can be disastrous. Under no circumstances should you try to twist the

Exam board	AQA	Edexcel	OCR	Eduqas
Paper/section	Paper 1 Section A	Paper 1 Section A	Paper 2 Section B	Paper 1 Section A
Type of question	Extract-based question requiring a response to an aspect of the extract and a response to **the same/similar** aspect in the **play as a whole.**	Two-part question: **Part (a)**: extract-based question requiring close response to language. **Part (b)**: question requiring a response about a **linked** theme **elsewhere in the play.**	*Either* an extract-based question requiring a response to an aspect of the extract and **the same** aspect in the **play as a whole.** *Or* an essay question requiring a response to the **play as a whole.**	Two-part question: **Part (a)**: extract-based question requiring a response to an aspect of the extract. **Part (b)**: essay response to a different aspect in the **play as a whole.**
Closed book?	Yes	Yes	Yes	Yes
Choice of question?	No	No	Yes – answer one question from a choice of two.	No
Paper and section length	**Paper 1:** 1 hour 45 minutes **Section A:** approximately 50 minutes	**Paper 1:** 1 hour 45 minutes **Section A:** approximately 55 minutes	**Paper 2:** 2 hours **Section B:** 45 minutes	**Paper 1:** 2 hours **Section A:** approximately 1 hour – 20 minutes on extract task, 40 minutes on essay
% of whole grade	20% Literature grade	25% Literature grade	25% Literature grade	20% Literature grade
AOs assessed	AO1: 12 marks AO2: 12 marks AO3: 6 marks AO4: 4 marks **Total = 34 marks**	**Part (a):** AO2 only: 20 marks **Part (b):** AO1: 15 marks AO3: 5 marks **Total = 40 marks**	AO1: 16 marks AO2: 18 marks AO3: 4 marks AO4: 2 marks **Total = 40 marks**	**Part (a):** AO1: 7.5 marks AO2: 7.5 marks **Part (b):** AO1: 10 marks AO2: 10 marks AO4: 5 marks **Total = 40 marks**
Is AO4 (SPaG) assessed in this section?	Yes	No	Yes	Yes – in Part (b) only

question to the one that you have spent hours revising or the one that you answered brilliantly in your mock exam.

Are you being asked to think about how a character or theme is presented or is the question about a description of a place? Make sure you know so that you are able to sustain your focus as you write.

As you can see from the table provided, all the exam boards offer *Romeo and Juliet* as a text and all offer an extract-based question. (Note that OCR offers a choice of two questions – the first uses an extract but the second is a discursive essay that does not provide an extract.) However, the wording and format of the questions are slightly different for each board. The extract will be linked to one or two tasks for you to complete.

As a starting point, you may wish to underline key words in the question, such as 'how' to remind you to write about methods, and other words which you feel will help you to focus on answering the question you are being asked.

Below you can see examples of the question types from each examination board which have been annotated by students in this way.

AQA

Starting with this moment in the play, explore how Shakespeare presents Romeo's relationship with the Friar.

Write about:

- how Shakespeare presents Romeo and the Friar in this extract
- how Shakespeare presents their relationship in the play as a whole.

Edexcel

(a) Explore how Shakespeare presents Romeo's relationship with Friar Lawrence in this extract.

Refer closely to the extract in your answer.

(b) In this extract, Romeo and Friar Lawrence talk about love.

Explain the importance of love elsewhere in the play.

In your answer you must consider:

- where love is shown
- how love affects those involved.

You should refer to the context of the play in your answer.

OCR

EITHER

Explore how the Friar's attitude towards Romeo influences events in the play. Refer to this extract from Act 2 scene 3 and elsewhere in the play.

OR

How and why do you think Juliet's relationship with the Nurse changes? Explore at least two moments from the play to support your ideas.

NB for OCR, the alternative essay question will not be related to the extract.

Eduqas

(a) Look at how Romeo and Friar Lawrence speak and behave in this extract. What does it reveal about their relationship? Refer closely to details from the extract to support your answer.

***(b)** How does Shakespeare present relationships between children and parents in *Romeo and Juliet*?

*5 marks are allocated to this question for accuracy in spelling, punctuation and the use of grammar.

NB for Eduqas, the second question will not be related to the extract.

Spot the differences!

- AQA and Edexcel divide their question into two separate sections, (a) and (b), which are related by the same or a similar aspect.
- AQA refers to **the play as a whole**.
- Edexcel and OCR use the phrase **elsewhere in the play**.
- Edexcel does not give marks to AO4 in this question.
- Only OCR gives you a choice of an extract-based question or an essay unrelated to the extract.
- OCR's first question option offers an extract for initial analysis and then as a springboard to analyse a related idea elsewhere in the play.
- OCR's second question option does not provide an extract but gives a discursive essay question instead.
- Eduqas has two separate questions – an extract question and an essay question.
- Eduqas does not test AO3 in this question.

Important: AQA, Eduqas and OCR assess both AO1 and AO2 in this section of the exam paper. Edexcel assesses AO2 in part (a). Always make sure you cover these AOs in your response, even if they do not seem to be signposted clearly in the question!

'Working' the text

- If you are answering all or part of a task based on an extract, your next step is to read the passage very carefully, trying to get an overview or general impression of what is going on, and what or who is being described.
- Next, read the extract again, underlining or highlighting any words or short phrases that you think might be related to the focus of

the question and are of special interest. For example, they might be surprising, unusual or amusing. You might have a strong emotional or analytical reaction to them or you might think that they are particularly clever or noteworthy.

- To gain high marks for an AO2 response, you have to consider how words and phrases may work together to produce a particular effect or to encourage you to think about a particular theme. You will need to explore the methods the writer uses to present a character in a particular way.

- You may pick out examples of literary techniques, such as lists or use of imagery, or sound effects, such as alliteration or onomatopoeia. You may spot an unusual word order, sentence construction or use of punctuation.

GRADE *BOOSTER*

When you start writing you must try to explain the effects created by particular words/phrases or techniques, and not simply identify what they mean. AO2, the Assessment Objective concerned with language, is worth a high proportion of the marks, so your answer will have to demonstrate your understanding of how Shakespeare's imagery, diction, rhyme and so on help to communicate the character's thoughts to the audience. Above all, ensure that you are answering the question.

Planning your answer

It is advisable to write a brief plan before you start writing your response to avoid repeating yourself or getting into a muddle. A plan is not a first draft. You will not have time to do this. In fact, if your plan consists of full sentences at all, you are probably eating into the time you have available for writing a really insightful and considered answer. A plan is important because it helps you to gather and organise your thoughts, but it should consist of brief words and phrases.

You may find it helpful to use a diagram of some sort – perhaps a **spider diagram** or **flow chart**. This may help you to keep your mind open to new ideas as you plan, so that you can slot them in. You could make a list instead. The important thing is to choose a method that works for you.

If you have made a spider diagram, arranging your thoughts is a simple matter of numbering the branches in the best possible order.

Note: if you are sitting the Eduqas exam, it is advisable to plan your essay response rather than the extract response.

GRADE *BOOSTER*

Examiners recognise that a plan is often a sign that a response will be good. Planning really can help to raise your grade.

Writing your answer

You are ready to start writing your answer. Remember you are working against the clock so it's really important to use your time wisely.

You may not have time to deal with all of the points you wish to make in your response. If you simply identify several language features and make a brief comment, you will be working at a fairly low level. The idea is to **select** the features that you find most interesting and develop your comments in a sustained and detailed manner.

You must also remember to address the whole question as you will be penalised if you fail to do so. For example, if the question asks you to consider character and relationship you must refer to both of them in your answer.

If you have any time left at the end of the examination, do not waste it! Check carefully that your meaning is clear and that you have done the very best that you can. Look back at your plan and check that you have included all your best points. Is there anything else you can add? Keep thinking until you are told to put your pen down.

Referring to the author and title

You can refer to Shakespeare either by name (make sure you spell it correctly) or as 'the writer' or 'the playwright'. You should never use his first name (William) – this sounds as if you know him personally. You can also save time by giving the play title in full the first time you refer to it, and afterwards simply referring to it as 'the play'.

> **GRADE** *BOOSTER*
>
> Do not lose sight of the playwright in your essay. Remember that the play is a construct - the characters, their words, their actions and reactions, have all been created by Shakespeare - so most of your points need to be about what Shakespeare might have been trying to achieve.
>
> In explaining how Shakespeare's message is conveyed to you, for instance, through an event, an aspect of a character, use of symbolism, personification, irony and so on, don't forget to mention him.
>
> For example:
> - Shakespeare makes it clear that…
> - It is evident from … that Shakespeare is inviting the audience to consider…
> - Here, the audience may well feel that the writer is suggesting…

Writing in an appropriate style

Remember that you are expected to write in a suitable **register**. This means that you need to use an *appropriate* style. You should:

- not use colloquial language or slang: 'Capulet is a right nasty piece of work.' (The only exception is when quoting from the text.)
- not become too personal or anecdotal: 'Mercutio is like my mate, 'cos he....'
- use suitable phrases for an academic essay. It is better to say 'It could be argued that...' rather than 'I reckon that....'
- not be too dogmatic. Don't say 'This means that....' It is much better to say 'This might suggest that....'

You are also expected to be able to use a range of technical terms correctly. The *Language, style and analysis* section of this guide should help with that. However, if you can't remember the correct name for a technique but can still describe its effect, you should still go ahead and do so.

GRADE *BOOSTER*

If you can't decide whether a phrase is a simile or a metaphor, it helps to just refer to it as an example of imagery.

The first person ('I')

It is perfectly appropriate to say 'I feel' or 'I think'. You are being asked for your opinion. Just remember that you are being asked for your opinion about *what* Shakespeare may have been trying to convey in his play (his themes and ideas) and *how* he does this (through characters, events, language, form and structure of the play).

Spelling, punctuation and grammar (AO4)

Most exam boards specifically target **spelling, punctuation and grammar** (SPaG) (AO4) for assessment in the Shakespeare question, except for Edexcel. The marks available may not be as high as for the other objectives, but you cannot afford to forget that you will demonstrate your grasp of the play through the way you write, so take great care with this. You will throw away marks if you make careless errors. Even worse, if the examiner cannot understand what you are trying to say, they will not be able to give you credit for your ideas, so accuracy matters.

GRADE *BOOSTER*

It is important to make the individual quotations you select brief and to try to **embed** them in your response. This will save you time, enabling you to develop your points at greater depth and so raise your grade.

How to raise your grade

- Answer the question which is in front of you. You need to start doing this straight away. When writing essays in other subjects, you may have been taught to write a lengthy, elegant introduction explaining what you are about to do. You have only a short time in the Literature exam, so get started as soon as you've gathered your thoughts together and made a brief plan.

- Sometimes students panic because they don't know how to start. It is absolutely fine to begin an extract-based response with the words, 'In this extract Shakespeare presents...' because whichever exam you are sitting, you need to start with the extract (unless you choose the discursive essay option in the OCR paper).

- Pick out interesting words and phrases, and unpick or explore them within the context or focus of the question. For example, if the question is about the way that conflict is presented, you need to focus on words and phrases to do with conflict.
  - What methods has the playwright used? It might be something as simple as a powerful adjective. What do you think is the impact of that word? It might be that the word you are referring to has more than one meaning. If that's the case, the examiner will be impressed if you can discuss what the word means to you, but can also suggest other meanings.
  - Is context relevant? For instance, would Shakespeare's readers view conflict differently? What might Shakespeare have been trying to express about conflict when he chose this word or phrase?

- It is likely that you will find it easier to address AO2 (methods) when writing about the extract as you have the actual words in front of you. However, do not be tempted to quote at length from the extract! It is also worth remembering that you need to show a range of understanding of the play. If you are sitting the Eduqas paper, do not rely heavily on the extract provided in part (a) when you tackle the separate essay in part (b). If you do, the examiner will consider that you do not know the play very well and are having to rely on the extract for your references.
  - Is there an overall effect? For instance, you may have noticed Shakespeare's frequent use of oxymorons in some characters' speeches. As well as analysing individual words in your extract (not necessarily all of them – just the most interesting ones) you could also describe the cumulative effect of having these oxymorons.

- Be very careful about lapsing into narrative, or writing about a character as if he or she is a real person. For example, if you are asked about how Shakespeare presents Romeo, remember that the focus of the question is about the methods that Shakespeare uses. Do not simply tell the examiner what Romeo does or what he is like – this is a very common mistake.

- Remember that AQA, Edexcel and OCR also ask you to deal with an aspect of the question related to the rest of the play, not just the extract. You will be penalised if you do not do this so you MUST leave time. If you feel you have more to offer in terms of comments on the extract, leave a space so that you can return to it if you have time.

GRADE BOOSTER

Beware! Some candidates might think extract questions look easy but some exam boards require you to show knowledge of other parts of the play as well as the printed extract, so make sure you leave enough time to write a full answer to the question.

Key points to remember

- Do not just jump straight in! Time spent wisely in those first moments may gain you extra marks later.
- Write a brief plan (not needed for Eduqas part (a) (extract) question).
- Remember to answer the question.
- Refer closely to *details* in the passage in your answer, support your comments and, where asked, remember that you must also refer to the play as a whole or refer to 'elsewhere' in the play.
- Use your time wisely! Try to leave a few minutes to look back over your work and check your spelling, punctuation and grammar, so that your meaning is clear and so that you know you have done the very best that you can.
- Keep an eye on the clock!

GRADE *FOCUS*

Grade 5

Students will have a clear focus on the text and the task and will be able to 'read between the lines'. They will develop a clear understanding of the ways in which writers use language, form and structure to create effects for the readers. They will use a range of detailed textual evidence to support comments. They will show understanding of the idea that both writers and readers may be influenced by where, when and why a text is produced (this point does not apply to Eduqas).

Grade 8

Students will produce a consistently convincing, informed response to a range of meanings and ideas within the text. They will use ideas which are well-linked and will often build on one another. They will dig deep into the text, examining, exploring and evaluating the writer's use of language, form and structure. They will carefully select finely judged textual references which are well integrated in order to support and develop their response to the text. They will show perceptive understanding of how contexts shape texts and responses to texts (this point does not apply to Eduqas).

Aiming for a grade 9

To reach the very highest level you need to have thought about the play more deeply and produce a response which is conceptualised, critical and exploratory at a deeper level. You might, for instance, challenge accepted critical views in evaluating whether the writer has always been successful. If, for example, you think Shakespeare set out to dispute the influence of fate over our actions, how successful do you think he has been?

You need to make original points clearly and succinctly and convince the examiner that your viewpoint is really your own, and a valid one, with constant and careful reference to the text. This will be aided by the use of short and relevant quotations, skilfully embedded in your answer along the way.

GRADE *BOOSTER*

Less successful answers will often consist of a series of unsupported points or superficial explanations. To aim for higher grades, work at your explanations. Show your ability to analyse ideas *and* features of style. Offer alternative interpretations where you can. This will help you to reach grade 8 or 9.

REVIEW YOUR LEARNING

1 On which paper is your *Romeo and Juliet* question?

2 Can you take your copy of the play into the exam?

3 Will you have a choice of question?

4 How long do you have to answer the question?

5 What advice would you give to another student about using quotations?

6 Will you be assessed on spelling, punctuation and grammar in your response to *Romeo and Juliet*?

7 Why is it important to plan your answer?

8 What should you do if you finish ahead of time?

Answers on p. 109.

Assessment Objectives and skills

All GCSE examinations are pinned to specific areas of learning that the examiners want to be sure the candidates have mastered. These are known as Assessment Objectives or AOs. The same Assessment Objectives apply to your response to *Romeo and Juliet* whether you are studying it as an examination text for AQA, Eduqas, OCR or Edexcel. The examiner marking your response will be using the particular mark scheme for that board, but all mark schemes are based on fulfilling the key AOs for English Literature.

Assessment Objectives

What skills do you need to show?

Let's break down the Assessment Objectives to see what they really mean.

> **AO1** Read, understand and respond to texts. Students should be able to:
> - maintain a critical style and develop an informed personal response
> - use textual references, including quotations, to support and illustrate interpretations.

At its most basic level, this AO is about having a good grasp of what a text is about, and being able to express an opinion about it within the context of the question. For example, if you were to say, 'The play is about the conflicting nature of love' you would be beginning to address AO1 because you have made a personal response. An **informed** response refers to the basis on which you make that judgement. In other words, you need to show that you know the play well enough to answer the question.

Closely linked to this is the idea that you are also required to **use textual references, including quotations, to support and illustrate interpretations.** This means giving short direct quotations from the text. For example, if you wanted to support the idea that Romeo can be violent, you could use a direct quote to point to this fact, such as Romeo's challenge to Paris, 'Wilt thou provoke me? Then have at thee, boy!' Alternatively, you can simply refer to details in the text, in order to support your views. So you might say, 'Romeo can be violent because he kills both Tybalt and Paris during the course of the play.'

Generally speaking, most candidates find AO1 relatively easy. Usually, it is tackled well – if you answer the question you are asked, this Assessment Objective will probably take care of itself.

> **AO2** Analyse the language, form and structure used by a writer to create meanings and effects, using relevant subject terminology where appropriate.

AO2 is not as easy as AO1. Most examiners would probably agree that covering AO2 is a weakness for many candidates, particularly those students who only ever talk about the characters as if they were real people.

In simple terms, AO2 refers to the writer's methods and is often signposted in questions by the word 'how' or the phrase 'how does the writer present…'.

Overall AO2 is easily overlooked, so it is vital that you are fully aware of this objective. The word **language** refers to Shakespeare's use of words. Remember that writers choose words very carefully in order to achieve particular effects. They may spend quite a long time deciding between two or three words which are similar in meaning in order to create the precise effect that they are looking for.

If you are addressing AO2 in your response to *Romeo and Juliet*, you will typically find yourself using Shakespeare's name and exploring the choices he has made. For example, looking at how Shakespeare has Capulet use violent verbs such as 'hang, beg, starve, die' when he threatens Juliet, will set you on the right path to explaining why these words are an interesting choice. It is this explanation that addresses AO2, whilst saying 'Capulet is cruel' is a simple AO1 comment.

Language also encompasses a wide range of the writer's methods, such as the use of different types of imagery, words which create sound effects, litotes, irony and so on.

AO2 also refers to your use of **subject terminology**. This means that you should be able to use terms such as *metaphor*, *alliteration* and *hyperbole* with confidence and understanding. However, if you can't remember the term, don't despair – you will still gain marks for explaining the effects being created.

The terms **form** and **structure** refer to the kind of text you are studying and how it has been 'put together' by the writer. This might include the use of a Chorus to provide an overview, the order of events and the effects created by it, and the way key events are juxtaposed. For example, Lady Capulet's announcement that Juliet is to marry Paris in two days' time follows Juliet's wedding night with Romeo. It thus offers a powerful contrast. Effects of structure can also be seen in Shakespeare's use of sentence lengths and word order (syntax).

Remember – if you do not address AO2 at all, it will be very difficult to achieve much higher than grade 1, since you will not be answering the question.

> **AO3** Show understanding of the relationship between texts and the contexts in which they were written.

Note: AO3 is not assessed in the *Romeo and Juliet* question in the Eduqas examination.

This AO, although perhaps not as important as AO1 and AO2, is still worth between 15% and 20% of your total mark in the examination as a whole, and so should not be underestimated. You need to check your exam board to see what proportion of the AO3 marks are given to the question on *Romeo and Juliet*.

To cover AO3 you must show that you understand the links between a text, the literary tradition to which it belongs and the writer's beliefs. For example, some awareness of honour in Elizabethan times might help you understand why Mercutio is so keen to fight Tybalt and defend Romeo's name. Equally, some knowledge of the Elizabethan belief in fate compared to Shakespeare's interest in free will might help you when assessing how far we can consider Romeo and Juliet victims of their decisions or of circumstance.

However, it is important to understand that context should not be 'bolted on' to your response for no good reason – you are writing about literature, not history!

> **AO4** Use a range of vocabulary and sentence structures for clarity, purpose and effect, with accurate spelling and punctuation.

Note: AO4 is not assessed in the *Romeo and Juliet* question in the Edexcel examination.

A clear and well-written response should always be your aim, even where no marks are given to this AO. If your spelling is so bad or your grammar and lack of punctuation so confusing that the examiner cannot understand what you are trying to express, this will obviously adversely affect your mark. Ensure that you can spell key words and character names, that your grammar, spelling and punctuation are clear and you structure your essay clearly.

Similarly, although there are no marks awarded for good handwriting, and none taken away for untidiness or crossings out, it is just as important that the examiner can read what you have written. If you believe your handwriting is so illegible that it may cause difficulties for the examiner, you need to speak to your school's examination officer in plenty of time before the exam. They may be able to arrange for you to have a scribe or to sit your examination using a computer. Note that the use of a scribe or computer can sometimes reduce your SPaG mark, according to whether you had spell check enabled or your scribe punctuated your work. You should speak to your school examination officer about the rules.

Common mistakes

You will not gain many marks for:

- **Retelling the story.** You can be sure that the examiner marking your response knows the story inside out. A key feature of the lowest grades is 'retelling the story'. Don't do it.

▲ Don't forget about the author!

- **Quoting long passages.** Remember, every reference and piece of quotation must serve a very specific point you are making. If you quote at length, the examiner will have to guess which bit of the quotation you mean to serve your point. Don't impose work on the examiner – be explicit about exactly which words you have found specific meaning in. Keep quotations short and smart.

- **Merely identifying literary devices.** You will never gain marks simply for identifying literary devices such as a simile or a use of rhyme. However, you will gain marks by identifying these features, exploring the reasons why you think the writer has used them and offering a thoughtful consideration of how they might impact on readers, as well as an evaluation of how effective you think they are.

- **Giving unsubstantiated opinions.** The examiner can give you marks for your opinions, but only if they are supported by reasoned argument and references to the text.

- **Writing about characters as if they are real people.** It is important to remember that characters are constructs – the writer is responsible for what the characters do and say. Don't ignore the author!

REVIEW YOUR LEARNING

1 How many Assessment Objectives (AOs) are there?

2 What does AO1 assess?

3 What sort of material do you need to cover to successfully address AO2?

4 What aspects of the text should you write about to gain AO3 marks?

5 What aspects of your writing does AO4 cover? Is it assessed in your *Romeo and Juliet* answer?

6 Which exam board specification are you following and what AOs should you be focusing on?

7 What should you **not** do in your responses?

Answers on p. 109.

Target your thinking

- What features does a grade 5 essay have?
- How does a grade 8 essay improve on that?
- What makes for a good introduction and conclusion?
- What is an 'appropriate' essay style?

Sample responses to two exam questions are provided below. (See *Tackling the exams* for information about the format of the examination.) The responses are from two students working at different levels. They cover much the same points. However, you should be able to see how Student Y takes similar material to that of Student X, but develops it further in order to achieve a higher grade.

AQA-style question and response

The question below is typical of the style of an AQA question which asks you to consider how a character or theme is presented in an extract and then, more generally, how it is presented in the play as a whole.

AQA advises you to spend about 50 minutes on this question.

Read the following extract from Act 3 scene 1 of *Romeo and Juliet*.

In this extract, Tybalt is challenging Romeo to a fight.

TYBALT

Romeo, the love I bear thee can afford

No better term than this: thou art a villain.

ROMEO

Tybalt, the reason that I have to love thee

Doth much excuse the appertaining rage

To such a greeting. Villain am I none;

Therefore farewell, I see thou knowest me not.

TYBALT

Boy, this shall not excuse the injuries

That thou hast done me, therefore turn and draw.

ROMEO

I do protest I never injured thee,

But love thee better than thou canst devise,

Till thou shalt know the reason of my love;

And so, good Capulet, which name I tender

As dearly as my own, be satisfied.

MERCUTIO

O calm, dishonourable, vile submission!

Starting with this extract, write about how Shakespeare explores conflict in *Romeo and Juliet*.

Write about:

- how Shakespeare presents the conflict between Tybalt and Romeo in this extract
- how Shakespeare explores conflict in the play as a whole.

[30 marks]

AO4 [4 marks]

Student X, who is likely to achieve grade 5, began the response with this introduction:

1 This shows some awareness of Shakespeare's craft in creating drama.

3 This does add a new point – that Romeo attempts to calm Tybalt down.

5 By preceding this quote with 'Romeo says he isn't a villain', quoting from the text has been made unnecessary as it's already been paraphrased. It would have been better to embed the quote by writing, 'Tybalt calls Romeo a villain, who disputes this with "Villain am I none".

> Shakespeare uses the threat of violence to create tension and excitement. In this scene, Romeo does not want to fight with Tybalt but Tybalt wants to fight with Romeo. Tybalt is trying to provoke Romeo but Romeo doesn't want to fight him and tries to calm him down. Tybalt calls Romeo a 'villain' but Romeo says he isn't a villain. 'Villain am I none' and he tries to walk away but Tybalt carries on winding him up.

2 A repetitive sentence. When making a character statement, a reverse statement on another character is not necessary.

4 A new point, but expressed in a repetitive way.

6 The phrase 'winding him up' is too informal for an exam answer.

On the surface, this is a sound enough start. It shows some awareness of the writer and goes on to outline the content of the scene. However, it is at present fairly limited in its approach.

Student Y, who is likely to achieve grade 8, wrote an introduction that addresses each of the Assessment Objectives. This is a *very* strong skill for an introduction. It is also done in A-level English so you know you're starting well if you can do it at GCSE.

1 The wider question – the theme of conflict – is addressed in the very first sentence. Examiners call this 'immediate engagement' and it is a great start!

2 The scene is set in place. Shakespeare's technique (to highlight the ever present threat of violence) is touched on, which gains marks in AO2. The content of the scene is covered succinctly – AO1.

> One of the main themes of 'Romeo and Juliet' is the impact of conflict upon society. The Prologue outlines the 'ancient grudge' and 'new mutiny' that will underpin the story. In the given extract from Act 3 scene 1, Shakespeare highlights the ever present threat of violence in the play, by presenting Tybalt's confrontation of Romeo. Any challenge to a man's honour at this time was regarded as a clear invitation to fight, so Romeo's refusal is startling to Mercutio.

3 Context is addressed – AO3. The introduction is well written – AO4.

Remember that an examiner does not assess your grade in the final sentence of the essay. It is a continuous process. A strong start signals to the examiner that you know what you're doing and are going to be presenting a strong argument.

Both students then went on to analyse the extract.

Student X wrote:

> Shakespeare shows Tybalt's desire for conflict when Tybalt says,
>
> 'Thou art a villain',
>
> which is a strong and provocative word. Romeo doesn't want to fight because he's just got married to Juliet in secret so now he's part of the Capulet family. He can't tell Tybalt about this because it's a secret, so he says,
>
> 'the reason that I have to love thee'
>
> but he doesn't tell him what it is.

1 This shows some awareness of the author's choice of Tybalt as the aggressor, but the point could be developed further, for example to describe the effect on the audience's sympathies.

2 The reason for Romeo's reluctance to fight is explained succinctly.

3 There is an attempt at embedded quotation, which is a strength. Context is hinted at. There is attention to language.

> Romeo says that most people would feel 'rage' to be called a 'villain' but he doesn't feel like that today. 'Rage' is a strong and emotive word that describes Tybalt more than Romeo. Romeo turns away from the fight and says
>
> > 'Therefore farewell'
>
> and he tries to walk away.

4 This is recounting what is happening rather than analysing. Also note the incorrect spelling of 'tries'.

Student Y wrote:

> The theme of conflict is highlighted immediately in Tybalt's opening words to Romeo – 'thou art a villain'. Romeo has just come from his marriage with Juliet and would be in a really positive mood, so this insult is a startling contrast to the happy atmosphere of the previous scene. Shakespeare juxtaposes atmosphere for the audience to illustrate that threats and violence are never far away in this society. It is also pertinent that the Friar hoped the marriage would turn the 'households' rancour to pure love', yet it has made no difference at all.
>
> Shakespeare presents irony for us in Tybalt's sarcastic words that 'the love' he has for Romeo is nothing, when the audience knows that Romeo is actually in love with Tybalt's cousin. The idea of true love against Tybalt's mocking words highlight the themes of love and hate in the play.
>
> Romeo obviously recognises that the 'appertaining' or expected reaction to an insult like Tybalt's would be 'rage'. Romeo is aware of the codes of society at this time and knows his honour is being challenged. Romeo echoes Tybalt's language and repeats the word 'love' back to him, but turns it back from sarcasm

1 Refers to the question again to show that the argument is on track.

2 Knows the play well. Looks at Shakespeare's craft. Clear understanding of this scene's role in the wider play.

3 A really sensitive point.

4 Analyses language. Links this to wider themes.

5 Quotations are used purposefully. Context is embedded.

to genuine feeling by speaking of 'the reason that I have to love thee.' There is further irony in Romeo's statement to Tybalt,

'I see thou knowest me not.'

> **6** Thoughtful language analysis.

On the surface, it just suggests that Tybalt doesn't understand the kind of calm man Romeo is trying to be, but the audience would also understand the second meaning, which is that Tybalt doesn't know Romeo is now related to him through marriage to Juliet.

> **7** Recognises different interpretations.

Both students then went on to write about Tybalt's second attempt to provoke Romeo.

Student X wrote:

Shakespeare makes it clear that Tybalt doesn't want to let his chance of a fight go and he calls Romeo 'Boy' which is insulting and would be even more insulting when the play is set because men didn't like their honour to be challenged.

> **1** Awareness of context.

> **2** This shows an awareness of Shakespeare's stagecraft in showing that conflict can be exciting.

Because Tybalt's first insult to Romeo didn't work, Shakespeare then raises the tension when Tybalt just tells Romeo to

'turn and draw'

> **3** Again, the explanation is brief.

meaning that he has to fight. Tybalt is a bad-tempered character. When he was at the Capulet party he wanted to fight Romeo for turning up when he wasn't invited, so this is now Tybalt's chance to get his own back.

> **4** Shows textual knowledge to strengthen point.

Romeo still refuses to fight. He explains,

'I do protest I never injured thee'

> **5** Tends to say 'this means' in explanation, which reduces interpretations rather than opens them to different ideas. There is some attention to language.

which means that he hasn't done anything against Tybalt. The word 'protest' is quite strong and shows that Romeo knows his own mind. Romeo hints at the reason why he is now a friend to Tybalt and says,

'And so, good Capulet, which name I tender

As dearly as mine own, be satisfied.'

He means that he is now married to Juliet so the Capulet family name is important to him. Shakespeare is using dramatic irony here because the audience knows the real reason even though Mercutio doesn't.

Mercutio is amazed that Romeo is taking all these insults and says,

'O calm, dishonourable, vile submission!'

He means that Romeo is just giving in to Tybalt and he can't believe it. This is why he fights Tybalt because he's sticking up for Romeo.

6 Explains with understanding.

7 This indicates a low grade 5. To move above this level, more explanation is needed and, in particular, more awareness of author.

Student Y also wrote about Tybalt's second attempt to provoke Romeo:

Shakespeare goes on to show how Tybalt continues to antagonise Romeo by addressing him as 'Boy', which is clearly patronising. Tybalt is seeing how far he can push Romeo before he retaliates. The insult would have been particularly marked in Veronese society at this time when a man's honour was dear to him. Tybalt is effectively brushing aside Romeo's attempt at reconciliation by saying that his words

'shall not excuse the injuries

That thou hast done me.'

This seems like a hyperbolic statement to a modern audience but Tybalt feels that his honour has been insulted by Romeo's attendance at the Capulet party. Tybalt would also feel further insult at the fact that, presumably, Romeo has not replied to the challenge he sent in a letter. Tybalt was humiliated by Capulet telling him that Romeo 'shall be endured' at the party and has waited for the chance to assert himself and re-establish his honour. Now that he is being robbed of this chance

1 Embeds context.

by Romeo's refusal to fight, he becomes increasingly angry.

2 Sensitive analysis. Evaluates character which is a top grade skill.

Tybalt demands that Romeo 'turn and draw'. He hasn't been able to coax him into a fight so Shakespeare has Tybalt use imperatives to demand conflict. This is not surprising to the audience as Tybalt has acted aggressively every time he has been on stage.

4 Effective character overview.

3 'Shakespeare has Tybalt use imperatives' recognises the writer's craft. Productive use of terminology.

Romeo's language is calming. Love for Juliet has softened his actions and given him patience in tense situations. Unfortunately, Romeo's explanation that he loves Tybalt 'better than thou canst devise' doesn't have the result of placating Tybalt but infuriates him further as Romeo's reason is not clear. It could also even be interpreted as implying that Tybalt is ignorant as he cannot 'devise' Romeo's meaning, although Romeo is unlikely to intend it to suggest this. Romeo's final words here, 'be satisfied', are a further attempt to calm but are likely to be received by Tybalt as a command, which would rile him further.

5 Explains character's motivations.

6 Considers interpretations.

At this point, Mercutio steps in, astonished that his friend is accepting these insults. The audience already knows that Mercutio is bothered by what he sees as Romeo becoming weakened by love. Earlier in the play, Mercutio implied that Romeo was not 'man' enough to tackle Tybalt, being 'run through the ear with a love song'. The metaphor suggests that love is Romeo's only focus now. Benvolio disagreed that Romeo was not up to a fight, saying 'he will answer … being dared' but it seems that Benvolio was wrong. Shakespeare uses this discussion of honour to highlight its importance in society. This explains

7 Wider reference to the play. Attention to technical devices.

Mercutio's willingness to step in and fight for Romeo's name.

8 Shakespeare's craft. Context is embedded.

The idea of the name is also explored in the given scene. Opposing names are central to the play's conflict. The hatred between Capulet and Montague is behind all of the violence we have seen so far. When Romeo says that Capulet is a

'name I tender

  As dearly as mine own'

he undermines the reasons for the years of fighting and proves how needless the conflict has been. This idea was explored by Juliet earlier, in her questioning 'What's in a name?', suggesting that Romeo has been influenced by Juliet's opinions.

9 Continues to keep the question in mind.

10 Really subtle reference to strengthen point.

The students then moved on to reference other parts of the play.
Student X wrote:

1 Sustains focus on argument.

Shakespeare presents conflict in a later part of the play when Capulet wants Juliet to marry Paris. Juliet has just spent the night with Romeo so it is even more of a shock to her when her mother comes to tell her that the wedding with Paris will be on Thursday. Juliet says,

  'He shall not make me there a joyful bride'

which infuriates her mother. 'Shall not' makes her sound definite. In Shakespeare's day it was usual for a father to decide who his daughter would marry. Lady Capulet does not stick up for Juliet. She says,

'I would the fool were married to her grave'

and this is ironic because that's what happens.

2 Shows textual knowledge. Purposeful use of quotation. Some attention to language.

3 Could embed more but relevant contextual point.

4 Some use of terminology. Textual knowledge.

5 Maintains focus on argument.

The conflict continues when Capulet has a go at Juliet. He says,

'doth she not give us thanks?'

because he can't believe it.

6 A supported point but it is undeveloped.

7 Purposeful textual selection. Could explain this point more.

He says that Juliet uses 'chopt-logic' which means that she doesn't make sense. He threatens to throw her out of the house which was usual in Shakespeare's time.

8 Evidence of context but it's rather sweeping. Take care with this.

Juliet's father calls her all sorts of things, like 'baggage' and 'minion'. The language shows that he is really mean with no respect for her as these words are insulting and suggest she is a thing rather than a person. He says that she can 'starve in the streets'. The scene shows that there is conflict within families and not just on the streets of Venice.

9 Textual selection. The last quotation isn't *quite* correct, although an examiner wouldn't be overly harsh about this.

10 Keeps the question in mind. Note that 'Venice' has been written instead of Verona. If you make a one-off slip like this, don't panic too much – it is unlikely to affect your mark.

The conflict is finally brought to an end by Romeo and Juliet killing themselves. The Prologue said that this would 'bury their parents' strife' and that is true because Montague and Capulet shake hands at the end, so Shakespeare shows resolution to the conflict.

11 The conclusion goes some way to drawing the argument together.

Note that the question asked the candidate to analyse conflict in the extract and *the play as a whole*. After the extract, it is only really Capulet's argument with Juliet that is analysed, with a quick reference to the play's conclusion. However, the argument is otherwise well structured. There is understanding of characters and their links to conflict are explored with some detail. Some effects are analysed. There is a range of textual evidence to support comments. Student X is showing an ability to achieve just into grade 5 with this clear, coherent response.

Student Y continued the response by looking at the consequence of Tybalt's challenge:

Mercutio retaliates with an insult of his own, calling Tybalt 'rat catcher' and using the dramatic verbs 'dry-beat' and 'pluck' to emphasise his violent intentions. When Mercutio is fatally wounded, he curses with, 'A plague a'both your houses!' to show his conviction that his injuries are due to the

1 Language analysis.

conflict between the two families. Romeo reflects on his role in the fight and regrets that his attraction to Juliet's beauty has made him 'effeminate' and 'softened valour's steel'. This presents Elizabethan male/female stereotyping to the audience, as acting calmly is seen to be a female trait and therefore something weak. Romeo then embraces conflict and swears that,

'fire-eyed fury be my conduct now!'

before he hastily kills Tybalt. The compound adjective emphasises the extent of his new anger and how he will convert it to violence. Minutes after declaring this though, Romeo regrets killing Tybalt and calls himself 'fortune's fool'. It is interesting that he doesn't seem to blame himself for his part in the conflict, but rather blames fate for making conflict happen.

Shakespeare does not only present conflict between enemies but shows us conflict between friends. In Act 3 scene 3, Romeo argues with the Friar. He has relied on the Friar as an advisor and confidante, but he rails against his banishment and accuses the Friar of being heartless.

'Thou cut'st my head off with a golden axe
And smilest upon the stroke that
murders me.'

Shakespeare has Romeo use the language of conflict, with the violent verbs 'cut'st' and 'murders'. The Friar's exclamatory tone in 'rude unthankfulness!' shows his anger with Romeo. The Friar accuses Romeo's tears of being 'womanish' and it is interesting that this is the same criticism as Romeo levied at himself for failing to protect Mercutio. Again, Shakespeare presents feminine qualities as undesirable, as an Elizabethan man would have wished to be regarded as strong and unemotional.

Margin annotations:

3 Purposeful textual support.

2 Flags up question to focus argument.

4 Embeds context.

5 Specific language analysis and accurate terminology.

6 A really sensitive point. Evaluative, which is a grade 8/9 indicator.

7 Widens scope of argument.

8 Closely read. Purposeful use of terminology.

9 Cross-reference shows that the candidate knows the text well. Embeds contextual point.

Shakespeare also shows us conflict within families when Capulet tries to force Juliet to marry Paris. Her refusal leads him to use the violent threats that he will 'drag' her to church. The theme of youth and age is also presented here as contributing to conflict because father and daughter cannot relate to each other. Capulet wants to hit Juliet and says his 'fingers itch' to strike her. However, when she is found apparently dead in Act 4, he is distraught and, in contrast to his many vocal threats earlier, finds that grief 'will not let (him) speak.' This shows the audience that conflict can lead characters to make threats in the heat of the moment.

Ultimately, conflict in the play leads to peace, as the lovers' deaths bury 'their parents' strife.' Even in peace, Shakespeare reminds us of the violence of the play, as he has the Prince say that heaven has found a way to 'kill ... joys.' The theme of conflict unites other themes, including love and hate, youth and age, friendship and enemies, but each ultimately leads to peace.

10 Widens scope of argument again.

11 Links characters to theme.

12 Evidence of sensitive personal response.

13 Confident conclusion that blends specific detail with overview.

This response covers all of the Assessment Objectives. The candidate analyses the extract in detail and then moves on to select appropriate evidence to build a wide-ranging, cohesive argument. The candidate moves from specific focus to wider overview, which shows real confidence with the text. These skills indicate a high grade 8 result.

Eduqas-style question and response

The question below is typical of the style of part (a) of an Eduqas question, in that it asks you to analyse an extract by itself. There will then be a *separate* essay question on a different theme or character (part (b)).

Eduqas advises you to spend about 20 minutes on the extract question.

Enter JULIET

JULIET

The clock struck nine when I did send the Nurse;

In half an hour she promised to return.

Perchance she cannot meet him: that's not so.

O, she is lame! Love's heralds should be thoughts,

Which ten times faster glides than the sun's beams,

Driving back shadows over low'ring hills;

Therefore do nimble-pinioned doves draw Love,

And therefore hath the wind-swift Cupid wings.

Now is the sun upon the highmost hill

Of this day's journey, and from nine till twelve

Is three long hours, yet she is not come.

Had she affections and warm youthful blood,

She would be swift in motion as a ball;

My words would bandy her to my sweet love,

And his to me.

But old folks, many feign as they were dead,

Unwieldy, slow, heavy, and pale as lead.

Enter NURSE (with PETER)

O God, she comes! O honey Nurse, what news?

Hast thou met with him? Send thy man away.

NURSE

Peter, stay at the gate.

Exit PETER

JULIET

Now, good sweet Nurse – O Lord, why look'st thou sad?

Though news be sad, yet tell them merrily;

If good, thou shamest the music of sweet news

By playing it to me with so sour a face.

NURSE

I am a-weary, give me leave a while.

Fie, how my bones ache! What a jaunce have I!

JULIET

I would thou hadst my bones, and I thy news.

Nay, come, I pray thee speak, good, good Nurse, speak.

NURSE

Jesu, what haste! Can you not stay a while?

Do you not see that I am out of breath?

JULIET

How art thou out of breath, when thou hast breath

To say to me that thou art out of breath?

The excuse that thou dost make in this delay

Is longer than the tale thou dost excuse.

Is thy news good or bad? Answer to that.

Say either, and I'll stay the circumstance:

Let me be satisfied, is't good or bad?

What does this extract show about Juliet's state of mind at this point in the play? Refer closely to details from the extract to support your answer. [15 marks]

Student X, who is likely to achieve grade 5, began the response like this:

1 A response to an extract does not need an introduction. You can say where the extract is from to set it 'in place' but should then move straight into your answer – you only have 20 minutes!

4 Correct use of terminology. Writing 'Shakespeare uses…' instead of 'Juliet uses…' would address AO2 more closely and improve this section.

'Romeo and Juliet' is a famous love story. I am going to look at Juliet's state of mind at this point in the play. Juliet is impatient to see the Nurse. 'The clock struck nine when I did send the Nurse' shows that Juliet has been watching the time. Juliet is worried when she says 'Perchance she cannot meet him' which has a big impact. Juliet's insult to the Nurse that 'she is lame!' shows Juliet's frustration and the exclamation mark emphasises this. Juliet uses a metaphor when she says that 'Love's heralds should be thoughts' to suggest that she wishes news from Romeo would come as quickly as she can think. Shakespeare uses adjectives in 'nimble-pinioned' and 'wind-swift' to suggest that Juliet's focus is all on how she wishes she could speed up time.

2 The student states Juliet's feelings. There is a clear structure to the point but not much explanation.

3 The phrase 'big impact' is vague. So far, this answer is not particularly strong.

5 There is explanation of effect to strengthen the response.

Student Y, who is likely to achieve grade 8, began the response like this:

1 The extract is set 'in place' succinctly.

This extract is taken from Act 2 when Juliet is waiting impatiently for news of Romeo from the Nurse. Shakespeare immediately emphasises time in the focus on 'the clock struck nine' and 'half an hour' to indicate that this theme will be an important concern to Juliet in this extract and indeed, to the play as a whole. Juliet's tendency to consider negative consequences is shown in her concern that 'Perchance she cannot meet him'. This idea illustrates that Juliet is a thoughtful character who weighs possible outcomes, an idea that is also echoed later in the play.

3 The question is kept firmly in mind.

The idea of trying to suppress negative thoughts follows in the idea that 'the sun's beams' can drive away 'shadows over low'ring hills'. The lexis 'shadows' and 'low'ring' sounds oppressive and indicates Juliet's concerned state of mind clearly.

The compound adjectives 'nimble-pinioned' and 'wind-swift' emphasise Shakespeare's precise language use and clearly emphasise Juliet's concentration on time. 'Nimble' is a stark opposite to the Nurse's slow return. Juliet craves a 'wind-swift' messenger, so there is humour in the 'a-weary' and 'out of breath' go-between that she actually has.

2 Writing 'Shakespeare immediately emphasises…' recognises the writer's craft and gains marks in AO2. Quotations are also used more selectively than they were by Student X. The phrase '…and indeed the play as a whole' widens the scope of the answer sufficiently, without drifting off to write about other areas of the play outside the extract.

4 There is specific language analysis.

5 The point is original and imaginative with close attention to language.

Both students then went on to consider the way that Shakespeare uses time to present Juliet's state of mind.

Student X wrote:

1 This point is structured clearly but only implies that Juliet wants time to pass and does not actually state this explicitly.

> Juliet means that it is midday when she says 'Now is the sun upon the highmost hill/Of this day's journey' showing that she has been waiting for the Nurse for three hours. She says this again in 'from nine to twelve/Is three long hours, yet she is not come'. This shows that she has been waiting much longer than she thought she would and is getting impatient. The 'long' hours emphasise this.

2 The point is made again but more specifically this time.

Student Y dealt with the same idea more effectively:

> Shakespeare evokes time effectively by telling the audience that the sun is on the 'highmost hill' of the 'day's journey'. This personifies the sun as a traveller and conveys that Juliet has waited 'long hours' to hear about Romeo's marriage intentions. The conjunction 'yet' further emphasises the Nurse's failure to return promptly.

1 Quotations are used selectively and purposefully. Terminology is used effectively in this original interpretation of Shakespeare's ideas.

2 Specific language analysis.

Both students then considered the idea of youth and age.

Student X wrote:

2 Another accurate point and the technique has been identified, although the brief explanation doesn't add much to what the student has already said.

> Juliet wishes that the Nurse was younger and more 'youthful' because then she could move more quickly. A simile is used when Juliet says the Nurse could be 'as swift in motion as a ball' showing that she wishes she was quicker.

1 This is an accurate point, if a bit straightforward.

The quality of the response suggests that the candidate is working at grade 5 and is demonstrating *clear understanding* by selecting appropriate textual references and, usually, explaining their effects.

Look carefully at what Student Y wrote about youth and age and note the differences between the two responses.

> The idea of passion is introduced when Juliet expresses a wish that the Nurse had 'warm youthful blood.' This illustrates Juliet's desire for Romeo, which is an idea built on later, prior to their wedding night. Juliet wishes that the Nurse was 'swift in motion as a ball' and the simile presents the hope that messages could be passed quickly between the lovers. The Nurse's age prevents her from doing this, which clearly annoys Juliet. The negative adjectives, 'Unwieldy, slow' and 'heavy', suggest that age is a burden. Juliet says that 'old folks' 'feign' as if they were dead, and the word suggests that the Nurse pretends to be older than she is because she enjoys fussing about her aches and pains. This suggests that Juliet is perceptive about the Nurse's character but can also be irritated by her.

1 This is an original and sensitive idea.

2 The effect of the technique is dealt with succinctly and confidently.

3 A short, focused point.

4 Alternative readings with clear attention to language.

This student is clearly writing at a higher level and is beginning to consider Shakespeare's methods in a thoughtful, developed style.

Both students then went on to write about the Nurse's return.

Student X wrote:

> Juliet is excited to see the Nurse, shown in the use of exclamation marks in 'O God, she comes!' and all the questions that Juliet asks. Juliet calls her 'good sweet Nurse' showing that she is being kind to her. The Nurse doesn't give any news for a long time. Instead, she complains about how tired she is and says 'I am a-weary.' She says that her 'bones ache' and she thinks Juliet should wait for the answer. The Nurse is 'out of breath.'

1 Tracks Juliet's state of mind with sound attention to techniques.

2 Could extend this point by addressing *why* Juliet is flattering the Nurse.

3 A common error has been made here. The student is starting to drift from the question which is about *Juliet's* state of mind. If this point had finished by tying the Nurse's lack of an answer to Juliet's growing annoyance, it would be more relevant.

97

Again, this answer shows *some* clear understanding, but there is room for improvement through more focus on the question. Student X finishes the response here. Juliet's last speech is not addressed. Although a conclusion is not needed in an extract response, it is not a good idea to ignore the final points of the extract and the examiner will be looking to see that you reach the end. However, the candidate has structured the answer well otherwise. There is understanding of character and some effects are described. There is a range of textual evidence to support comments. Student X is showing an ability to achieve just into grade 5 with this clear, coherent response, although it would benefit from greater attention to AO2.

Now read the next section of Student Y's response:

> Juliet's prediction that old people almost enjoy fussing about age comes true when the Nurse finally returns. Unlike her usual garrulous self, the Nurse says very little at first, showing that she is enjoying keeping Juliet waiting. The suspense is clearly frustrating Juliet, who asks a lot of questions that the Nurse doesn't answer. The Nurse is making the most of her moment of power. Juliet attempts to get an answer by flattering the Nurse, calling her 'honey Nurse', 'good sweet Nurse' and 'good, good Nurse'. The repetition conveys Juliet's desperation. Her hopefulness is shown in the comment that she is expecting 'the music of sweet news' that the Nurse is spoiling with her 'sour' face. The Nurse's continued delay encourages Juliet to stop asking questions and instead demand 'I pray thee speak' which shows that Juliet is losing patience.

1 The opening sentence links to the student's previous point, showing the control in this response.

2 The student shows confident character knowledge and ties this to the question.

3 Technique and effect are linked thoughtfully.

4 This is a subtle point.

5 The student is tracking Juliet's behaviour closely.

This response is sensitive and closely read. To improve even further, the fact that Shakespeare has Juliet use these techniques could be emphasised, so that the writer's craft is brought to the forefront of the response.

Student Y ended the response like this:

> Juliet's patience is tested further when, as she anticipated, the Nurse delays news by complaining about her aching bones and the 'jaunce' she's had, presenting the exhausting effort she thinks she's made. The effect this has on Juliet is to increase her impatience.
>
> Juliet makes the reasonable point that the Nurse is using her breath to complain when she could have told Juliet the news by now. Shakespeare does this to illustrate Juliet's ability to be logical, even in a stressful situation, which anticipates her behaviour later in the play. Juliet boils her questions down to the simple 'Is thy news good or bad?' and repeats this again 'is't good or bad?' in the hope that the Nurse can at least give her a one word answer. This shows that Juliet is trying to manage the situation. The audience learns a lot about Juliet's youthful enthusiasm and ability to act logically in this extract.

1 Ties the Nurse's behaviour to the effect on Juliet.

2 Presents Shakespeare's craft to gain marks in AO2.

3 Makes a really sensitive and evaluative character point.

4 An extract answer does not require a conclusion but the candidate ties this response up nicely with a brief character overview.

Throughout the answer, Student Y sustains a convincing, sensitive response which covers all the requirements to achieve grade 8, and possibly higher.

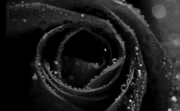

Top ten

Top quotations

As your examination will be 'closed book' and you will only have a short extract in front of you, you might find it helpful to memorise some short quotations to use in support of your points in your examination response, particularly when addressing the question about the rest of the play. See *Tackling the exams* for further information about the format of the examination.

You don't need to memorise long quotations; short quotations that you can embed into a sentence will be more effective. If all else fails, as long as you can remember the gist of what the quotation relates to, you can use a textual reference.

Top characterisation quotations

The following quotations can be used as a quick reminder of the way that Shakespeare has presented the key characteristic of each of the main characters.

Romeo

1 'Away from light steals home my heavy son,/And private in his chamber pens himself.' (1.1 128–129)

- Montague's words reveal that Romeo's parents are concerned about his secretive behaviour. The verbs 'steals' and 'pens' suggest a secretive nature.

2 'Verona brags of him/To be a virtuous and well-governed youth.' (1.5 66–67)

- Capulet explains that Romeo is known as a moral, respectful youth.

3 'O serpent heart, hid with a flow'ring face!/Did ever dragon keep so fair a cave?/Beautiful tyrant, fiend angelical!' (3.2 73–75)

- On hearing the news of Romeo's murder of Tybalt, Juliet contrasts Romeo's attractive appearance with his violent tendencies. The compound adjectives convey her depth of feeling.

Juliet

'O, she doth teach the torches to burn bright!/It seems she hangs upon the cheek of night/Like a rich jewel in an Ethiope's ear...' (1.5 43–45)

4

- Romeo watches Juliet at the party and uses a simile to praise her beauty.

'But soft, what light through yonder window breaks?/It is the east, and Juliet is the sun.' (2.2 2–3)

5

- Romeo uses a metaphor to highlight his attraction to Juliet.

'Hang thee, young baggage, disobedient wretch!/I tell thee what: get thee to church a'Thursday,/Or never after look me in the face.' (3.5 160–163)

6

- Capulet uses emotive language and violent threats to persuade Juliet to marry Paris.

GRADE *BOOSTER*

If you are a visual learner, you might try drawing a cartoon with the quotation as a caption.

Mercutio

'O then I see Queen Mab hath been with you:/She is the fairies' midwife...' (1.4 53–54)

7

- Mercutio tells Romeo that his dream was due to Queen Mab – the bringer of dreams. The lively language and pace conveys his imaginative nature.

'Ask for me tomorrow, and you shall find/me a grave man. I am peppered, I warrant, for/this world. A plague a'both your houses!' (3.1 89–90)

8

- Mercutio uses a pun about his imminent death. This turns to a curse as he lays blame for his death firmly at the feet of the Montagues and Capulets.

Nurse

'Go, counsellor,/Thou and my bosom henceforth shall be twain.' (3.5 239–240)

9

- Juliet has lost all faith in the Nurse and swears never to trust her again.

Friar

10 'I do spy a kind of hope,/Which crave as desperate an execution/As that is desperate which we would prevent.' (4.1 68–70)

- Juliet's desperate desire to avoid marriage to Paris leads the Friar to come up with an equally desperate and risky plan.

Top thematic quotations

Love

1 'O brawling love, O loving hate,/O any thing of nothing first create!' (1.1 167–168)

- This can apply to Romeo's confusion over his unreciprocated feelings for Rosaline and also to the brawls resulting from the feud.

2 'Is love a tender thing? It is too rough,/Too rude, too boist'rous, and it pricks like thorn.' (1.4 25–26)

- Romeo disputes Mercutio's ideas about love.

'It is too rash, too unadvised, too sudden,/Too like the lightning...' (2.2 118–119)

3

- Juliet's simile expresses her wariness at the speed with which the relationship with Romeo is developing.

Fate and free will

'my mind misgives/Some consequence yet hanging in the stars...' (1.4 106–107)

4

- Romeo senses that fate will work against him if he attends the Capulet party.

'O Fortune, Fortune, all men call thee fickle;/If thou art fickle, what dost thou with him/That is renowned for faith?' (3.5 60–63)

5

- Juliet personifies Fortune (fate) saying that it changes its mind a lot so will tire of keeping Romeo and surely send him back to Juliet soon. This is ironic. She never sees him alive again.

Friendship and enemies

'From ancient grudge break to new mutiny,/Where civil blood makes civil hands unclean./From forth the fatal loins of these two foes/A pair of star-crossed lovers take their life.' (Prologue 3–6)

6

- The plot of the play is neatly summarised.

'My only love sprung from my only hate!/Too early seen unknown, and known too late!' (1.5 137–138)

7

- Juliet's exclamatory tone conveys her distress at discovering Romeo's family background.

'For this alliance may so happy prove/To turn your households' rancour to pure love.' (2.3 91–92)

8

- The Friar hopes the lovers' marriage will bring peace. Ironically, it does.

Families

9 'My will to her consent is but a part.' (1.2 17)
- Capulet seems a modern parent for his time, apparently willing to let Juliet decide if she'd like to marry Paris or not.

10 'Sir Paris, I will make a desperate tender/Of my child's love: I think she will be ruled/In all respects by me....' (3.4 12–14)
- This is an ironic statement. Unbeknown to Capulet, his daughter is already married to Romeo.

Top moments in *Romeo and Juliet*

These quotations highlight plot points and will help you to gain an overview of the play.

1 'Three civil brawls, bred of an airy word,/By thee, old Capulet, and Montague,/Have thrice disturbed the quiet of our streets...' (1.1 80–82)
- The Prince reveals that fresh arguments keep starting from something as petty as an 'airy word'.

2 'Did my heart love till now? Forswear it, sight!/For I ne'er saw true beauty till this night.' (1.5 51–52)
- Romeo rejects his earlier obsession over Rosaline and falls in love with Juliet at first sight.

3 'If I profane with my unworthiest hand/This holy shrine, the gentle sin is this,/My lips, two blushing pilgrims, ready stand/To smooth that rough touch with a tender kiss.' (1.5 92–95)
- Romeo speaks to Juliet for the first time and offers a kiss.

4 'O Romeo, Romeo, wherefore art thou Romeo?/Deny thy father and refuse thy name;/Or if thou wilt not, be but sworn my love,/And I'll no longer be a Capulet.' (2.2 33–36)
- Juliet wishes Romeo would reject his family name. If not, she will reject hers for his love.

5 'If that thy bent of love be honourable,/Thy purpose marriage, send me word tomorrow.' (2.2 143–144)
- The relationship is progressing quickly. Juliet is the first one to mention the idea of marriage.

'"Tybalt is dead, and Romeo banished."/That "banished", that one word "banished",/Hath slain ten thousand Tybalts.' (3.2 112–114)

6

- Juliet considers that the impact on her of Romeo's banishment is far greater than that of Tybalt's death.

'Wilt thou be gone? It is not yet near day:/It was the nightingale, and not the lark,/That pierced the fearful hollow of thine ear.' (3.5 1–3)

7

- The morning after the lovers' wedding night, Juliet tries to persuade Romeo that it is not time for him to leave.

'O bid me leap, rather than marry Paris,/From off the battlements of any tower.' (4.1 77–78)

8

- Juliet's desperation to avoid marriage with Paris is clear.

'Eyes, look your last!/Arms, take your last embrace!' (5.3 112–113)

9

- Romeo says a last farewell to Juliet before killing himself.

'Go hence to have more talk of these sad things;/Some shall be pardoned, and some punished.' (5.3 307–308)

10

- The Prince reflects on the tragedy.

Non-fiction

- *Shakespeare: The World as a Stage* by Bill Bryson
- *Shakespeare's Words: A Glossary and Language Companion* by David Crystal and Ben Crystal
- *Shakespeare on Toast: Getting a Taste for the Bard* by Ben Crystal
- *1599: A Year in the Life of William Shakespeare* by James Shapiro
- *Contested Will: Who Wrote Shakespeare?* by James Shapiro

Useful websites

Your exam board website is a valuable resource for you to find sample exam questions and mark schemes, even sample answers like those in this guide. These resources are not just there for teachers – check out these links:

- AQA – http://aqa.org.uk/subjects/english/gcse/english-literature-8702
- Eduqas – http://eduqas.co.uk/qualifications/english-literature/gcse/
- Edexcel – http://qualifications.pearson.com/en/qualifications/edexcel-gcses/english-literature-2015.html
- OCR – www.ocr.org.uk/qualifications/gcse-english-literature-j352-from-2015/

Other useful websites include:

- Shakespeare Birthplace Trust – www.shakespeare.org.uk/home.html
- Shakespeare Online – www.shakespeare-online.com
- Shake Sphere – www.shakespearestudyguide.com
- The Royal Shakespeare Company – www.rsc.org.uk/education/online-resources/
- Absolute Shakespeare: *Romeo and Juliet* – http://absoluteshakespeare.com/guides/romeo_and_juliet/romeo_and_juliet.htm

Answers to Review your learning questions

Context (p. 15)

1 Context means the social, historical and literary factors that influenced the playwright.
2 The Prologue captures the audience's attention and makes events clear.
3 Both leaders had unquestionable power.
4 A contemporary called him an 'upstart crow', a fellow playwright (Ben Jonson) killed someone in a duel, quarrels over honour were not unusual.
5 A patriarchal society is one where women are of lower social status than men.
6 Most Elizabethans believed that God or fate controlled you – the opposite of free will and personal responsibility.
7 The Renaissance
8 Courtly love demonstrated men's attraction to unattainable women, like Romeo's attraction to Rosaline. Romeo moves on to find true love.

Plot and structure (p. 34)

1 The lovers are 'star-crossed'.
2 Romeo has heard it all before and is tired of the fighting.
3 The Capulets seem considerate, suggesting that Juliet shouldn't marry too young.
4 Mercutio is vivacious, making crude remarks when Romeo speaks of love. However, their Act 2 scene 4 jokes suggest a similar sense of humour. Mercutio is more willing to fight than Romeo.
5 The Prologue tells the audience that the lovers' relationship is moving forward quickly.
6 Juliet thinks their relationship is 'too rash, too unadvised, too sudden'.
7 Juliet's parents are seen as unrelenting and cruel.
8 The Friar agreed to marry Romeo and Juliet quickly.
9 The Prince
10 The Prologue outlined the lovers' deaths and the families' reconciliation and this is borne out in the final scene.

Characterisation (p. 46)

1 Adjectives to describe Romeo include: emotional, impulsive, lovesick, withdrawn and, later, more quick-witted. He is reckless at the play's end.
2 Adjectives to describe Juliet include: protected, beautiful, enthusiastic, thoughtful, courageous and a bit manipulative.
3 Tybalt
4 Tybalt

5 Juliet first mentions marriage when she says, 'If ... Thy purpose marriage.' (2.2 145)
6 Friar Lawrence and the Nurse
7 Romeo
8 The death penalty
9 The Nurse
10 An apothecary in Mantua

Themes (p. 53)

1 A theme is an idea which the writer explores through plot, structure, characterisation and description.
2 The main themes in *Romeo and Juliet* are: love and relationships, fate and free will, youth and age/parents and children, friendship and enemies, families and conflict.
3 Romeo, Juliet, Rosaline, Paris, the Friar (warns against haste in love but still marries the lovers), Mercutio (references sexual love), the Nurse (references sexual love), Capulet and his wife (arranged marriage)
4 Families, conflict and different views of love might also be explored.
5 Benvolio and the Friar
6 Conflict and families might also be explored.
7 The Prince admits to 'winking at' (turning a blind eye to) some of the families' 'discords' (5.3 294).
8 This is personal interpretation. However, the strength of Shakespeare's works is that his ideas are still concerns we have today.

Language, style and analysis (p. 66)

1 The comic moments highlight the later tragedy and convey a sense of chaos.
2 The Chorus is a bridge between actors and audience. It offers a commentary on events and focuses the audience's attention.
3 Imagery is visually descriptive language that literally creates an 'image'.
4 A sonnet
5 Benvolio
6 'The sun, for sorrow, will not show his head.'
7 Low rank characters speak in prose. High rank characters speak in poetry to show their importance and intelligence.
8 The oxymorons convey Romeo's confusion over his love for Rosaline.
9 'For here lies Juliet, and her beauty makes,/This vault a feasting presence full of light' (5.3 85–86) shows the impact Juliet's beauty has on Romeo.
10 Crude language creates humour for the audience. The double meanings lend comic ambiguity.

Tackling the exams (p. 76)

1 Paper 1 for AQA, Edexcel and Eduqas. Paper 2 for OCR.

2 All exams are closed book, so you cannot have your copy of the play with you.

3 There is no choice of question in the AQA, Edexcel and Eduqas papers. There is a choice of two questions in the OCR paper.

4 AQA – 50 minutes; Edexcel – 55 minutes; OCR – 1 hour; Eduqas – 1 hour (20 minutes on the extract, 40 minutes on the essay).

5 Quotations support points. They need not be long, and ideally should be embedded in your work.

6 Spelling, punctuation and grammar (AO4) is assessed in the Shakespeare exam section for AQA, OCR and Eduqas but not for Edexcel.

7 A plan will help you to organise your thoughts and avoid a muddle.

8 You should check your work to make sure that you have done your very best.

Assessment Objectives and skills (p. 81)

1 There are four Assessment Objectives.

2 AO1 assesses your understanding of the text and your ability to support your ideas with evidence.

3 AO2 requires comment about how the writer uses language, form and structure to create effects.

4 AO3 refers to the relationship between texts and the contexts in which they were written.

5 AO4 refers to the accuracy of spelling, punctuation and grammar. AQA, Eduqas and OCR give marks for AO4.

6 The AOs you should you be focusing on in the Shakespeare section of the exam are:

AQA	Edexcel	OCR	Eduqas
AO1 AO2 AO3 AO4	(a) AO2 (b) AO1, AO3	AO1 AO2 AO3 AO4	(a) AO1, AO2 (b) AO1, AO2, AO4

7 Do not: re-tell the story, quote at length, simply identify devices without explaining their effects, offer unsupported opinions or write about characters as if they were real.